OWN IT!

Take Charge of Your Career:

DEVELOP YOUR PERSONAL BRAND AND SUCCEED IN A CROWDED MARKET THROUGH PROFESSIONAL DEVELOPMENT, STORYTELLING AND NETWORKING

TUESDAY A. STRONG

To Gary, my iyuha.

"Be the change you wish to see in the world."

Mahatma Ghandi

Table of Contents

Acknowledgements

This book has been a labor of love built upon the inspiration of so many wonderful people. My husband Gary—you are my everything. Your love and support gives everything meaning and makes it all possible. I am grateful to my friend and mentor Jean Prather, who has always supported me and served as the consummate professional and teacher; and to my friend Julie Lunsford for her steadfast friendship and example. I wish to thank my family, Les and Sandy Boyle, for reminding me to laugh and enjoy life—I treasure you both. I'm indebted to my teachers: Saint Mary-of-the-Woods College for providing me with the inspiration to aspire higher; Indiana University and the Kelley School of Business for accelerating my educational and professional journeys and for introducing me to the concept of personal branding; and to Marc Dollinger who encouraged me to pursue my goals. My heartfelt thanks goes out to the professionals who read my blog and have asked the questions that inspired me to write this book.

Introduction

I wrote this book because times have changed. Market forces, employment trends and the pace of change have accelerated over the past few years. I participated in a personal branding program a couple of years ago offered by Indiana University and I realized the concepts in the program paralleled my human resources and marketing experience, training and beliefs. I've long been a believer that as professionals we are responsible for our professional development and for staying current with market conditions and employment trends. I shared information and connected with others as I worked to develop my personal brand. I began receiving requests for assistance and invitations to speak on personal branding. I then set out to discover the most effective way to scale up and share information with as many professionals as possible, and this book was the result.

OWN IT! was designed as a workbook—a practical workbook you can use to develop goals and a personal brand development plan that you can use. This workbook is organized to provide you with a brief overview of personal branding, and then guide you through a process of reflection, discovery and goal setting. A persona is used in the examples throughout the book to demonstrate how plans can be developed. You may want to read through the workbook prior to completing the exercises. Doing so will give you an overview of the material and how it can result in the creation of a personal brand development plan. This workbook was created to provide you with the understanding and tools to realize results.

Contact me at Tuesday@TuesdayStrong.com and share your feedback. For more tips and a free toolkit visit http://TuesdayStrong.com.

1

What Is Personal Branding?

Goals:

Chapter Goal:

1. Familiarize professionals with personal branding.

Reader Goal:

1. Understand the basic elements of personal branding.

1 What Is Personal Branding?

Technology, globalization, and the pace of change continue to be drivers for independent career management. Professionals too often rely on their employers to manage their careers. Feedback and professional development opportunities from the work environment are extremely valuable. They can help align your efforts, leverage your strengths, and improve your weaknesses, while helping you maintain or exceed performance expectations. But if you rely on such feedback and professional development opportunities in isolation you may be doing your career and long-term plans a disservice. Have you assumed responsibility for your career? Are you letting your employment situation dictate your focus? Or do you simply tell yourself you're too busy to add anything more to your schedule? If you are not proactively managing your career, don't be surprised when you're not promoted or considered for vacancies or other opportunities.

> "Your personal brand is your reputation."

For the majority of jobs it's no longer realistic to believe that anyone will be in any one position for several years, let alone for the life of their career. Yes, there are professions that are exceptions (physicians, attorneys and others). Work environments and the way in which we work and think about work continue to change at an accelerated pace. Career management is also changing. Savvy professionals are realizing that they are responsible for their careers and professional development. Owning your professional development means that you are responsible for making decisions about it. While this can work quite effectively when connected to the professional development opportunities provided by your workplace, it also ensures that you have a long range, comprehensive and flexible plan for your development that positions you for success in your current and future positions. Depending upon your goals, it may be necessary to invest in development that your employer isn't positioned to support.

Like it or not, perceptions are often reality, and they impact employment opportunities whether you seek a new job, want to keep your current position or advance within your existing organization. What can you do to influence perceptions if you want others to perceive you as a professional with just the right experience, education, and abilities? The answer to this question resides in understanding how others perceive you and how their perceptions were developed. Reputations are formed from interactions and perceptions. Your personal brand is your reputation. Every interaction others have with you and how they feel about you helps create your personal brand. All interactions are opportunities to build or detract from your brand. Reputation management, personal marketing, and other terms are used interchangeably with personal branding. Personal branding is about communicating how you can add value, and highlighting how you are unique. Personal branding is not about falsely promoting yourself. It is about using communication, perspective-taking, networking, and social media to develop and enrich relationships.

We have numerous opportunities throughout each day to develop our personal brands. From the moment we engage with others in person or online, our brands are strengthened or negatively impacted. This means that every text, post, email and conversation means a great deal if you're interested in ensuring that others know how you have added value or how you're uniquely qualified to add value in a variety of different contexts. Think about the interactions you have with others and how you feel about the interactions you have with them. Your perception influences your inclination to seek out opportunities to interact with them in the future. Equally important is to remember that every interaction others have with you creates positive, negative, or indifferent impressions about you for them.

> "Personal branding can help you get noticed in a crowded job market or in your current work environment, improve communication and build relationships."

Simple actions we take influences others' perceptions of us and impacts the likelihood that they will choose to interact with us in the future if given the choice. For example, purchasing a cup of coffee for someone you just met at your workplace leaves an impression with them. Were you considerate, rude, or indifferent? Did you leave a tip? Did you interrupt the waiter? Did you use basic manners? While this example may seem simple, its significance is noteworthy because each of us send messages that impact others' perceptions of us. These interactions and perceptions combine over time to create our reputations and personal brands. You can take steps to proactively communicate with others once you recognize the importance of interactions, perceptions, and branding and work to stop sending mixed or unintentional messages. Now think about how you would act if you met with a recruiter for a cup of coffee. In this situation you would most likely be quite aware of how you interact with him. How would your behavior differ if you were having coffee with a co-worker instead of a recruiter? You are most likely aware that you are leaving impressions in both situations, but the extent to which you make an effort to influence perception differs based upon your goals.

Increasing your awareness of your behavior, others' perceptions and how you add value for others are essential to developing your personal brand. Personal branding can help you get noticed in a crowded job market or in your current work environment, improve communication and build relationships. For someone to hire you or recommend that someone else does, people need to know you and like you; both of which are impacted by your ability to communicate how you can add value. They need to "know you and like you to pay you". In your current work environment you are known for many things based upon the interactions you've had with others and their perceptions of you. Do their opinions and perceptions align with what you want to be known for? Either way, you have work to do to ensure you're known for who you are (your values), what you've accomplished, and your capabilities.

Begin by understanding how others perceive you and how their perceptions were developed. Your personal and professional history should be leveraged to help tell your brand story. Consider how often job seekers attempt to match their experience, skills, and abilities with the requirements in a vacancy announcement. If you do this, do not think you are positioning yourself to stand out from the numerous cover letters and resumes received by recruiters. Yes, you should ensure you meet position requirements and include industry keywords. But what makes you unique will most likely attract attention, so it's critical to be able to communicate your compelling value proposition through a variety of mediums. Personal branding can positively impact a job search. It can be useful whether you want to keep your current position or transition to a new position. You communicate your personal brand by what you do, how you communicate, and with the choices you make each day. For job seekers, personal branding can help you get noticed in a crowded market. Personal branding at the most basic level involves your story, your brand identity, and social media.

Your Story

Your story is the foundation for developing your compelling value proposition, which demonstrates how you are uniquely qualified for a position or opportunity. Your story should tell:

- how you are different;
- how you add value;

- how you arrived at where you are today (creating an emotional connection); and

- where you are going (describing your goals in a broad sense).

Your Brand Identity

How you express yourself both verbally and visually is your brand identity, and how you communicate impacts your success connecting with others. The choices you make also send messages to others about who you are and what you value. This can involve everything from the company you keep to what you wear and the technology you use. Your brand identity can be leveraged to remind others of who you are and how you can add value, as well as to help differentiate you from others and draw attention to your unique qualities.

Social Media

How you use social media both personally and professionally impacts your personal brand. Every post, tweet, instant message, photograph and video that you add and comment that you make influences others' perceptions of you. The range and impact of social media can be profound and long lasting. Every action you take online using social media can spread throughout the Internet and be modified or taken out of context. Some professionals struggle with which social media platforms to use personally and which ones to use professionally, and others blur the lines between the two by sharing both personal and professional information with everyone they're connected with online. Be cautious if you seek to develop your personal brand and you communicate personal information with your professional networks.

Be aware of your 'digital footprint' and know of any incorrect or negative information online. This is important for both professionals who seek a new role with a different employer, as well as for individuals who want to stay with their current employer. A simple "Google®" or other online search can provide you with the type and scope of information available about you. You may also want to consider that many recruiters, employers, colleagues and others will Google® you to learn more about you either before or after meeting you. If you discover inappropriate or incorrect information about yourself on the Internet you should take action to have it removed if possible. You may need the help of professionals to remove or manage the information depending upon the circumstances and your goals. Go ahead and "Google®" yourself if you've not done so recently. Did you find information that represents you as a professional? Would you be comfortable with a recruiter or your employer viewing your personal Facebook® page? Do you even appear in search results? Not appearing in search results can leave negative impressions with recruiters and organizations as well. Not appearing in search results can mean that you are not current with technology, networking or social norms. You should appear on the first page of search results with links to current information about who you are, what you do and how you can be reached. You should be able to be reached through various sites without posting your contact information directly. A professional photograph or "head shot" should appear when others search for you. For many a simple search by a recruiter or other professional is the first impression they will have of you.

This workbook was created to be a practical tool to help you understand personal branding and how to create a personal brand development plan. I use a process of assessment, reflection, and decision to guide the development of your personal branding goals. Assessment helps you understand your story, preferences and performance. Reflection encourages you to think about your performance and activities to date in the context of your goals, assets and constraints. The decision sections are designed for you to document what you plan to do moving forward to achieve your goals. Let's get started!

2

Why Personal Branding Matters

Goals:

Chapter Goal:

1. Raise awareness of job seeker and recruiter practices.

Reader Goal:

1. Appreciate why personal branding is relevant for employed professionals, job seekers and recruiters.

2 Why Personal Branding Matters

During the past few years the job market has changed considerably and we have no choice but to change how we manage our careers and employment transitions if we are to survive and thrive in these new times. Work environments and the way in which we work and think about work will continue to be impacted by technology and a host of other factors. The challenge for most professionals is that they are too focused on doing what needs to be done in the short term, instead of discovering ways to manage their time and responsibilities so they can complete what needs to be done in the short term while taking action toward realizing longer-term career goals.

Change is a requirement even for professionals who want to stay in their current position. Few professional positions will go untouched by progress, given the global evolution of industries and economies. Digital norms and the continued infusion of technology into workplaces will make it necessary for professionals to frequently upgrade technology-related skills. Current job holders may find themselves competing with incoming talent, assuming the newly-secured talent is prepared to contribute in technology-driven work environments. Consider a hypothetical circumstance in which an employee who has used the same systems, equipment and processes for the past ten years with only one year of experience using recently implemented methods, systems and technology decides to apply for a promotion, while an employee with one year of experience using the organization's recently implemented new methods, systems, technology and processes also applies for the same vacancy. Now factor in that the employee with one year of experience at the company also has five years of experience with one of the company's main competitors who uses current methods, systems and technology. This type of situation occurs more and more frequently, and creates a need for employees to own their development and proactively seek opportunities to upgrade their skills and learn about technological advances and how they impact their company and their company's competitors.

> "Organizations want and seek adaptable employees."

The extent to which you pursue learning opportunities independent of your employer also indicates your level of commitment to your development. For some, it may not have been necessary to pursue continued learning and development independent from their employer, given the essential functions of their position. But by being able to provide evidence of your continued development you are expressing not only a commitment to development but also a willingness to change. This combines with the initiative you've shown in addition to the actual knowledge or skills you've gained from the content you studied. Lifelong learning is an investment that can be beneficial in many ways, and should be included in your personal and professional development plans.

Personal branding can be an effective means for showcasing your expertise or "thought leadership". Actively participating in professional associations and communities can be beneficial for the individuals you interact with and for your career. If you are currently employed, your employer can benefit as well. When you engage with others you are essentially representing your employer and their brand. In these situations you can add value for your employer's brand, detract from it, or simply fail to have an impact. Recruiters and organizations are increasingly recognizing the importance of employees as representatives of their brands—employees as brand ambassadors. By being an effective and valuable brand ambassador for your employer you are communicating to others, including recruiters and other organizations, that you could effectively represent other brands. Your effectiveness in this area in large part depends upon your understanding of your employer, its history and aspirations. These combine with your ability to communicate effectively and to represent your employer appropriately in various settings. You can find more information about brand ambassadors at http://tuesdaystrong.com. I foresee brand ambassadors becoming more common as organizations continue to discover new ways to differentiate themselves from their competitors.

Your online and in-person networks also contribute or detract from your personal brand. Most of us recognize the importance of our contacts and networks to our careers and personal satisfaction. Savvy professionals invest time, energy and money to develop and enrich their networks even when they are not pursuing a new job or other opportunity. The richness of your network is a reflection of you and your willingness to invest in and support others. Your communication skills and history are important to your personal brand, employability and career longevity, given that all organizations want employees who interact effectively with others. Keep this in mind as you review your social media networks and the extent to which you engage personally and professionally. The nature of the engagement, frequency and depth of content are also indicators of your communication style, preferences and practices. Developing your network both online and in person should be critical components within your personal and professional development plans.

The employment situation in recent years and continued global development have increased interest in how best to compete for employment. Competition has been so fierce in many fields for several years now that many are opting for jobs that can meet their most basic needs compared with the pursuit of lifelong progressive careers. The times in which we now work require new approaches for securing employment and developing careers. One new approach involves personal branding, where professionals focus on developing their ability to communicate using advanced techniques, storytelling and social media to describe how they can add value to organizations and others. This new employment era is transforming how individuals search for positions and how organizations select, retain and develop talent. It is no secret that talent is attracted to the best brands and organizations continue to compete for the best talent. What may not be as widely known is that a few basic techniques can help professionals manage their reputations and communicate their value to potential employers using consistent messaging across numerous platforms online and in person.

Successful job seekers continue to use networking and progressive methods to attract attention and stand out from others. I cannot emphasize enough the importance of in-person networking prior to and during job searches. Today's job seekers understand that the job search methods of the past are in large part no longer relevant. Social media and applicant tracking systems have changed how individuals locate and apply for positions. Well-connected job seekers can secure positions without applying for advertised vacancies, using networking, instead, to locate new opportunities. Future advances in technology will also impact the employment process and give job seekers a reason to stay current both with the process and with constantly evolving job search techniques.

Understanding Job Seekers

While a targeted relationship-based approach to securing a position is ideal, it's not always possible. If you seek a new position, it may be beneficial for you to better understand the techniques that other job seekers are currently using. Many job search websites allow job seekers to post resumes that are viewable to the general public without password or other protection. As of this writing, Indeed.com® is one such job search engine. Indeed.com® is an excellent resource for job seekers. While many use this site to search for positions, these same job seekers may overlook the ability to use Indeed.com® to determine how many job seekers are located in the area in which they are interested, and how these job seekers are presenting their qualifications. Try it for yourself. Go to www.indeed.com® and click "resumes". Enter a zip code or other parameters and links to job seeker resumes will appear. You can tailor search results by education, years of work experience, job titles, etc. Understanding how and where job seekers present themselves can be quite useful if you seek a new position. Many professionals supplement their in-person efforts with online networking. According to research by comScore Inc., Google® takes most job seekers to Indeed.com®, with Indeed.com® capturing 62 % of total job seeker traffic in January 2013.

While we continue to see an increase in job seekers using LinkedIn®, what is more interesting are the increases that we are seeing in individuals using Facebook® and Twitter® to find jobs. According to a 2012 Jobvite® Social Job Seeker Survey:

- **61%** of job seekers say finding a job has gotten harder in the past year;

- **41%** of employed job seekers are overqualified;

- **88%** of job seekers have at least one social networking profile; 64% have two profiles and 44% have three; and

- **1 in 6** job seekers credit social media for their current job.

The Market Matters

Fast forward to 2013 and the numbers warrant even greater attention from job seekers and employed professionals. Recruiters are using social media to locate and learn about both active and passive candidates. Understanding where recruiters are locating candidates can help you position yourself to be at the right place at the right time. Passive candidates who seek to maintain active profiles and grow networks on various social media channels should also be aware of the increase in recruiter activities.

According to the 2013 Jobvite Social Recruiting Survey which polled 1,600 recruiting and human resources professionals, 93% of recruiters are likely to look at a candidate's social profile. From this survey we discovered that the top social networks for recruiting in 2013 were LinkedIn® at 94%, Facebook® at 65% and Twitter® at 55%. Proactively and professionally managing your online profiles and interactions is important to your current position and to your career and future given that 78% of recruiters surveyed have made a hire through social media, and that 94% of recruiters use or plan to use social media in their recruitment efforts.

Establishing and maintaining a professional presence online can help recruiters screen you for vacancies. Your online presence and personal brand can provide a glimpse into your interests, experience, knowledge, skills, abilities and accomplishments. Your online presence can help you stand out among other potential candidates who possess comparable credentials and interests. While having a recruiter view your profile can have a positive effect, remember that any inappropriate content or images they discover will make a negative impression.

Your credibility is a key component of your personal brand, and requires that you actively communicate how you add value for others and provide, or be ready to provide, examples of past performance that demonstrate what you've done and the results realized. You should strive for consistency in the messages that exist on various social media sites. You should strive to add value to others so much so that it becomes a cornerstone of your persona. Equally important is tailoring your messages so they are appropriate for each site and audience. A lack of customization can indicate that you are more interested in broadcasting your message and not so much interested in adding value for others. Supporting and connecting others is important as well. The purpose of social media is to engage socially and not just send out one-way messages. In time you will most likely discover that by helping others you have actually helped improve your credibility and reputation. While this may initially appear counterproductive to any goals you may have of promoting yourself, it can be effective because you will become known as someone who promotes not just themselves, but as someone who provides value for others.

3

Your Professional Development

Goals:

Chapter Goals:

1. Demonstrate progressive goal setting techniques and self-directed personal and professional performance assessments.

Reader Goal:

1. Understand how to reflect upon past performance and develop goals.

3 Your Professional Development

Economic conditions and technology are reshaping professionals' career choices and work environments. This reshaping has intensified pressures for many professionals who are striving for work/life balance. For some, the notion of work/life balance is not possible with work dominating most days even during personal time. This situation has resulted in new ways of managing how we live and work, including how we pursue new opportunities. To develop a personal brand development plan that's in alignment with your goals, begin by understanding your level of satisfaction with your past performance.

Personal Assessment

Proactively assessing our personal and professional goals and performance periodically helps us learn how to achieve our goals and obtain fulfillment in both our personal and professional lives. Reflect upon the past year and place an "X" in the appropriate box in the table on the next page, to rate yourself in the categories that apply to you, adding categories as necessary. This exercise helps you quickly assess where you are concentrating your efforts, and offers a tool for identifying the areas in your life that you may want to focus on improving. The "expectations" are yours, and refer to the extent that you are satisfied with yourself in these areas. For a more comprehensive assessment, ask others to complete both the Personal and Professional Assessments on your behalf.

Category	Does Not Meet Expectations	Meets Expectations	Exceeds Expectations	Comments
Mind (Learning, Intellectual Stimulation, etc.)				

Category	Does Not Meet Expectations	Meets Expectations	Exceeds Expectations	Comments
Body (Health & Wellness)				
Spirit (Recognize & Connect)				
Family				
Friends				
Community				
Fun				
Fulfillment				
Financial				
Has a reputation for adding value				
Other				
Observations:				

Reflection—Personal Assessment

What are the top five areas in which you are exceeding expectations?

1. _____

2. _____

3. _____

4. _____

5. _____

What are the top five areas in which you are not meeting expectations?

1. _____

2. _____

3. _____

4. _____

5. _____

What are the top five areas that have been the most enjoyable or rewarding for you?

1. _____

2. _____

3. _____

4. _____

5. _____

Professional (Job and/or Career) Assessment

Similar to the Personal Assessment exercise, reflect upon the past year and place an "X" in the appropriate box in the table to rate yourself in the categories that apply to you, adding categories as necessary. This exercise helps you quickly assess where you are concentrating your efforts, and offers a tool for reflecting upon areas in your life that you may want to focus on improving. The "expectations" are yours, and apply to the extent that you are satisfied with yourself in these areas. For a more comprehensive perspective you may want to ask others to complete both assessments on your behalf. You may want to include ratings from a recent workplace performance evaluation. The goal is to obtain a well-rounded perspective of your performance.

Category	Does Not Meet Expectations	Meets Expectations	Exceeds Expectations	Comments
Job Knowledge				
Relationships (Team Player)				
Communication Skills (Includes how effectively you communicate your value)				
Productivity				
Quality				
Attendance				
Follows Policies/Procedures				
Leadership or Management				
Saves/Makes Money				

Category	Does Not Meet Expectations	Meets Expectations	Exceeds Expectations	Comments
Confident with a Dose of Humility				
Problem Solver (Creative)				
Proactive				
Other				
Observations:				

Reflection—Professional Assessment

What are the top five areas in which you are exceeding expectations?

1. _____

2. _____

3. _____

4. _____

5. _____

What are the top five areas in which you are not meeting expectations?

1. _____

2. _____

3. _____

4. _____

5. _____

What are the top five areas that have been the most enjoyable or rewarding for you?

1. _____

2. _____

3. _____

4. _____

5. _____

Consider the ways in which you can leverage your strengths now that you've completed the self-assessments and have an idea of the areas in which you'd like to improve. Too often we focus so much on improving our weaknesses that we overlook the ways in which we can use our strengths to achieve even more progress. We also tend to forget to celebrate our accomplishments. This is so easy for overcommitted professionals and workaholics to do because they are already working on what must be achieved next. What is it all for if we can't enjoy it? Yes, improve your weaknesses; but also leverage your strengths.

Professional development plans can be quite useful in managing your career. They can help align your efforts and resources with your goals. Professional development plans do not need to be complicated or take considerable amounts of your time. Making them useful involves your willingness to be adaptable and update them periodically. Using professional development plans has served me well for the past fifteen years while I completed my education, worked full-time, and strived to maintain a balance in my family, work and developmental time. Discover what works for

"Discover what works for you— what's important is having goals that you're actively working toward."

you—what's important is having goals that you're actively working toward. Goal setting and realization can be addictive, especially if you are a self-motivated individual who appreciates making progress. You may discover that as you reach goals, you are inspired to "raise the bar" and set even more challenging goals than what you just achieved. I am convinced that goals can be realized with the right amount of hard work, determination and support. Professional development plans are never completely final. They need updating periodically to ensure alignment with your goals and resources. Realizing your goals can also be a tremendous amount of fun. Be realistic and try not to be discouraged. Setbacks will occur, and you may need to re-evaluate and change your plans. Use the space provided to list your current professional development goals (independent of your work environment). Then refer to the next example and use the template to create objectives, strategies and tactics for achieving your professional development goals.

_____

_____

_____

_____

_____

_____

_____

_____

_____

_____

Professional Development Example

GOAL	OBJECTIVES	STRATEGIES	TACTICS	EFFORT EXPENDED	FOCUS ON RELATIONSHIPS
Accomplishment to be achieved.	Specific, measurable steps that have a completion date.	The "thinking" aspect involved in achieving your objectives.	The "doing" aspect involved in achieving a strategy.	Amount and quality of effort put forth.	Frequency and richness of engagement.
PROFESSIONAL DEVELOPMENT					
Obtain a Social Media Professional Certificate.	Complete the online self-paced program by 1 Nov.	Identify the ways in which a certificate in social media can impact my personal and professional goals.	Enroll in the program by March 1.	Complete course requirements before and after work and on the weekends.	Engage with my instructor and classmates on a regular basis. Connect on social media and stay in touch after we complete the program.
Be an active volunteer for the local Boys and Girls Club.	Begin volunteering by1 June.	Identify the ways in which I can use my talents to the benefit of the Boys and Girls Club and the children that aligns with my current career goals.	Meet with the volunteer coordinator and explore all of the options.	Meet during my lunch hour and after work.	Connect bi-weekly with the coordinator until I begin volunteering and weekly thereafter.
Maintain professional certifications not supported by my employer.	Complete bi-annual certification requirements by 1 Nov..	Explore alternate ways for achieving certification credits (e.g., serving as an instructor/other).	Compare certification requirement options with my capacity and goals.	Review, decide on and pursue credits on the weekends.	Reach out to my peers who hold the same certification and ask how they earn credits.

GOAL	OBJECTIVES	STRATEGIES	TACTICS	EFFORT EXPENDED	FOCUS ON RELATIONSHIPS
Gain new knowledge, skills and abilities unrelated to my current position.	Determine the demand for a new local networking meet-up group by 1 Aug..	Identify the ways in which a local networking meet-up group could be beneficial to various groups throughout the community.	Research and meet with professionals throughout the community to understand what groups exist, what's been successful and what hasn't worked.	Research before and after work and meet during lunch and after work as necessary.	Update my connections periodically regarding the progress of this initiative.

Professional Development Template

GOAL	OBJECTIVES	STRATEGIES	TACTICS	EFFORT EXPENDED	FOCUS ON RELATIONSHIPS
Accomplishment to be achieved.	Specific, measurable steps that have a completion date.	The "thinking" aspect involved in achieving your objectives.	The "doing" aspect involved in achieving a strategy.	Amount and quality of effort put forth.	Frequency and richness of engagement.
PROFESSIONAL DEVELOPMENT					

4

Who Are You?

Goals:

Chapter Goal:

1. Guide the discovery and self-reflection process.

Reader Goals:

1. Discover or re-affirm my values and passions and
2. Understand my knowledge, skills and abilities and constraints in relation to my career plans.

4 Who Are You?

Many of us go through the various exercises throughout our careers to "discover" what we're drawn to and what we're good at. The process of knowing yourself begins with understanding what positions you to be the most content and productive. The following exercise may help you know yourself better. Remember:

- *Values* define what is valid and important to us in life;
- *Passions* excite and fulfill us;
- *Knowledge* is a body of information that is acquired over time;
- *Skills* are what we can do;
- *Abilities* are special talents or personal qualities that impact our performance; and
- *Constraints* are factors that limit us. For example, you may lack the knowledge, skills or abilities to work in a particular field, and you may need additional training or experience to remove the constraint. For others, constraints could involve traveling within limited distances or working certain hours due to other obligations.

Identify Your Work/Career Related Values

Values are principles that motivate our decisions. Understanding your values will help you focus on career objectives that you will find fulfilling. When we are in positions that align with our values we are typically more content, productive and fulfilled. When this happens, it can be a win-win for both employees and organizations. Everyone's values are different. What is important is that you are aware of your values in relation to your ideal job or career.

Circle the values that resonate with you and use the space provided to enter additional values.

Work/Career Related Values		
Work directly helps others	Work with the public	Leadership has integrity
Work is challenging	Job/assignment rotations	Employee ownership/stock options
Diversity/global involvement	Work in a highly creative environment	Control the work of others
Work in teams	Be recognized for my contributions	Position offers excitement/risk-taking
Have authority to make decisions	Mission resonates with me	Work independently
Have stability and little change in duties	Work/life balance a reality	Family friendly
Focused on production	Respect for equality	Career paths
Professional development opportunities	Focus on health and wellness	Emphasis on people, profits and planet

Rank Your Work/Career-Related Values

List your top preferred values to have in a work environment or career. Place an "X" in the ranking that resonates with you. Use the space provided to add values and rank them. This exercise helps you identify what values are important to you even if they are not present in your current work environment.

Value	Not Important	Very Important	Essential
Ex. Work directly helps others			X
Ex. Leadership has integrity			X
Ex. Focus on health and wellness		X	

What are the top five values you seek to maintain or have in a work environment?

1. _____

2. _____

3. _____

4. _____

5. _____

Discover Your Passions

Our passions are what excite and fulfill us—they are what "lights our fire". It's important to understand your passions, and to discover if you can incorporate your passions into your work. Work is easier if you are passionate about what you do. Discovering your passions isn't always easy, but there are several steps you can take to begin the process. First, think about what kind of life will make you happy. It's easier if you begin with this in mind and then work to build that life, tapping into your passions as much as possible. Answer the questions below to discover more about your passions.

What makes you happy?

_____

_____

_____

What do you like to do in your free time?

_____

_____

_____

What would you do if salary and benefits were not factors?

_____

_____

_____

What are your hobbies?

_____

_____

_____

If you could write your own job description what would you write?

_____

_____

_____

You may want to think about the elements of your current position that you most dislike. This may help you recognize what parts of your work you enjoy. You may also want to ask your family and close friends their opinions regarding your passions. Lastly, consider your achievements over the past few years and identify areas in which you are particularly pleased about your accomplishments or involvement.

List your five main accomplishments during the past three years. Which of these excited you the most?

1. _____

2. _____

3. _____

4. _____

5. _____

These exercises should have helped you identify a few of your passions. If not, check online for additional resources and tools. Don't feel frustrated or pressured to discover your passions. Passions can be cultivated, so try new things and you'll quickly discover more about your likes and dislikes. Remember, our passions change over time, so don't be surprised when you or others close to you change their interests and invest their time, energy and money to develop new passions.

Understand Your Knowledge, Skills and Abilities

Understanding your knowledge, skills and abilities is important when creating both your professional development and personal branding plans. Most positions have minimum requirements for the knowledge, skills and abilities that applicants must meet in order to make it through an initial screening process prior to being selected for interviews.

Your knowledge, skills and abilities are critical to your employability and longevity in the workforce. Common definitions of these include:

- Your *knowledge* is what you have learned over time through education or experience;

- your *skills* are what you can do and can often be measured by tests; and

- your *abilities* are the special talents or personal qualities that enable you to perform observable tasks or activities.

By maintaining an awareness of your knowledge, skills and abilities, you can proactively manage your development and have a greater influence over your performance and success in the work force. A brief review of your knowledge, skills and abilities can help you better understand your strengths and weaknesses. You can use this information when you develop your story, social media profiles and talking points. Your goal involves positioning yourself to be an obvious choice for opportunities. Equally important is leveraging this information when talking with others who can be bridges to employers or other opportunities. You should be able to communicate confidently about your strengths and weaknesses, demonstrate how they have contributed to your prior successes, and how you are currently developing as a professional. Organizations often use these terms as if they are interchangeable. But they are unique, and having a thorough understanding of the terms and of your knowledge, skills and abilities will be beneficial to your professional success. Work through the following exercises to better understand your knowledge, skills and abilities.

Do you have experience in a particular field? If so, for what length of time?

_____

_____

_____

_____

Describe the scope of your responsibilities. Did you work independently or on teams? Did you oversee the performance of others?

_____

_____

_____

_____

_____

Describe your experience as it relates to your role and the knowledge you have acquired.

_____

_____

_____

Describe your formal education. List any degrees, majors, specialties or training from which you've acquired knowledge.

_____

_____

_____

List the interpersonal, mental and physical skills you have acquired that you would prefer to continue to use (e.g., communicating to individuals and large groups in person and online, managing information, leading teams through challenging circumstances, etc.).

_____

_____

_____

Describe your abilities (e.g., use creativity to create new products and services, conceptualize inventions, self-motivate to achieve goals, etc.).

_____

_____

_____

Constraints

Certain conditions can limit or prevent you from achieving your personal branding goals. Depending upon your circumstances, some constraints may be foreseeable and preventable. Identifying and planning to avoid, reduce or eliminate the impact of preventable constraints should be included in your personal brand development plans. For example, you may develop personal branding goals that include having professionally-created brand identity materials, e.g., website, brochure, logo, business cards, etc., that are currently not financially feasible. You could opt to add professionally branded materials into your plans at a later date when you have budgeted and saved for them, or you could determine how you will increase your income (. obtain a part-time job or second source of income), to support your goals within your original time period.

Time, support, and lack of awareness or understanding can also be constraints whose impact you may want to prevent or offset. Timing can be a challenge for most of us. It's easy to assume more responsibilities than we have time to realistically manage, let alone to devote time, on a consistent basis, to our professional development and personal branding plans. If you work full-time and help manage a household, in addition to volunteering or serving within your community, you may cringe at the thought of adding more items to your "to do" list or plans. But devoting time, money and energy to your professional development and personal brand can be worth the investment in both the short and long term. If your schedule is already full or overcommitted, you may need to re-evaluate your priorities and resources and develop a plan that incorporates learning and personal branding. Both learning and personal branding can be achieved on a budget and with dedicated minimal amounts of time.

Planning is important to help guide you, but it's important to remember and even anticipate that circumstances may necessitate that you abruptly change your plans. You may need to readjust and then resume them at a later date. This happened to me when I began my MBA program a few years ago. I started with a plan to achieve two degrees in a very aggressive time frame while working full-time. I knew I could manage working full-time and going to school because I'd developed the work and study habits over the previous few years, having completed two other programs under similar circumstances. What I hadn't anticipated involved my assisting with the care of a family member who became very ill just as I started the program. After evaluating my situation and the likelihood of my success, I decided to take a six month break from my studies and re-take a course. While I was very discouraged at the time, since I'd not had to re-arrange my goals before, I learned to better manage set-backs.

Everyone can benefit from strong support systems. Family, friends, mentors, peers and others associated with your goals can offer support and encouragement. While goals and support levels differ, you can anticipate welcoming support if you have full-time obligations and commit to achieving new goals that require additional time, funding and energy. Saying no to others can be a challenge because we live in a society that has impressed upon us that we can "do it all" or "have it all". This attitude can influence us to assume responsibility for more than we can realistically handle, which can result in a great deal of stress or stress-related problems.

Another factor that can impact your progress toward achieving personal branding goals involves a lack of awareness or understanding of market conditions, norms or trends. Understanding market conditions is critical to the longevity of any career. If you lack an

> "You must proactively manage your health if you want a successful career."

awareness of market conditions, you have several options to get up-to-date and stay current. Independent research may be the most viable option for you because you can learn when your schedule permits and make inquiries when you have the time. Depending upon your level of awareness and understanding, you could begin by learning about your organization's history and products or services, the industry, its competitors and partners, locations, financials, plans, leadership, resources and which regulations impact its operation. Secondary research could involve meeting with your peers, leadership and mentors to learn more and discover additional sources of information.

Your health could also be a constraint to realizing your personal branding goals. You are actually limiting or preventing your professional success if you fail to manage your health and be an active participant in your wellness. Health and wellness are critically important to our careers because without them we function at lower levels, if at all. You must proactively manage your health if you want a successful career. You know if you are proactively managing your health and wellness and if devoting more time and resources are necessary.

You may be someone who is challenged by change and you may not be emotionally ready to change. Your level of commitment will impact your level of success. If you do want to develop your personal brand but you are someone who gets stressed at the thought of change, try identifying the cause of your stress and deciding if you can work to eliminate it or offset its effects. Perhaps you are already aware of the source of your stress and have decided that you will work to manage it because you know this is just part of your personality— that's good because you know you will have to take steps to manage it while you make progress toward your goals. If this is the case, draft

> "Remember that personal branding does not need to involve a great deal of money— you can actually begin without investing any money by focusing on free resources or by enhancing your current activities and access."

your personal brand development plan and select a few of the goals to work on in the short term. Then review your progress and update your goals and plans. You may find it easier (and less stressful) to work on a few goals at a time, rather than goals from each category. The key is to determine your goals and work toward them while reflecting upon your progress from time to time and updating your plans as necessary.

Another constraint that some professionals experience involves their digital footprint. You may be able to delete information that's no longer relevant but depending upon your circumstances you may need assistance from professionals with expertise in reputation management. Other constraints that impede or limit progress can involve distance, time and funding. If you are unemployed or underemployed you may find that funding is the greatest challenge for you. Remember that personal branding does not need to involve a great deal of money—you can actually begin without investing any money by focusing on free resources or by enhancing your current activities and access. For example, you can set up or update profiles on various social media sites and focus on both in-person and online networking. You could also use a no or low-cost provider for setting up a webpage or blog to display content that you have created. The goal is not to strive for something fancy or elaborate (unless this is what you want to be known for) but rather to be professional.

List five constraints with the potential to impact your personal branding plans.

1. _____

2. _____

3. _____

4. _____

5. _____

Examples include:

- Time
- Money
- Health
- Lack of awareness or understanding
- Less than optimal digital footprint

List five potential actions you could take to prevent, remove or offset the impact of the constraints you identified.

1. _____

2. _____

3. _____

4. _____

5. _____

Examples include:

- If time were a constraint you could re-prioritize your personal and professional goals using weighted criteria.

- If money were a constraint you could reduce your expenses, increase your income or use a combination of both.

- If your health were a constraint you could add wellness and health to your goal planning and set both short and long term goals.

- If a lack of awareness or understanding were a constraint you could identify individuals, groups and sources that could help improve your awareness on a consistent basis.

- If you need to clean up your digital footprint, you could seek assistance from professionals with expertise in reputation management.

5

Prepare to Tell Your Story

Goals:

Chapter Goal:

1. Demonstrate how to develop a professional story

Reader Goal:

1. Recognize how my story can impact my personal brand.

5 Prepare to Tell Your Story

The Value of Your Story

Your story should help others understand what makes you unique. Your uniqueness can attract attention—attention that leads to opportunities. The events in your life, the jobs you have held and the impact you have had on the lives of others have been integral in your development. They do not describe who you are, but instead connect to create a journey that is your life, and that has resulted in the person you have become. Your uniqueness resides in the person you are now. Sharing your story with others helps them understand how you view the world and how you developed your views. Your story can also help others understand how you can add value to their lives.

> "Your goal for sharing your story is to establish and strengthen relationships."

Your goal for sharing your story is to establish and strengthen relationships. This can happen if you share your history, current situation and your aspirations. Sharing in this way can help others understand how you arrived at who you are today as well as offer a glimpse into how you may act in the future. Your story should be told with a positive tone using emotion selectively. If possible, include a pivotal moment in your life and how this event influenced you. Once you have captured your story you can edit it for both in-person and online situations. The creation of your story enables you to develop themes, key words and talking points that you can use consistently over time to help reinforce your brand identity and build brand equity. You want others to hear your name or see your photo and instantly associate words and meaning with you.

Writing Your Story

Your history, current situation and future aspirations should be the main elements in your story. Telling your story begins with understanding your history and identifying elements that describe your accomplishments, potential and aspirations. The way in which you describe important events can impact the extent to which others relate with your story. How others perceive and welcome the information you share depends in large part on how you describe the pivotal moments in your life. Everything you share should be described in a positive tone. Your story should use clear and concise language and help others understand what you stand for, who you are and what you're capable of.

> "Your uniqueness can attract attention— attention that leads to opportunities."

Answer the questions included in this chapter and then invest time in developing your story. If this is challenging for you, develop a draft that you can go back and refine after you've read the remainder of the workbook and gained a better understanding of how the workbook can help you develop your personal branding plans. Your story should contain an opening, a foundation, your current situation and vision, or future aspirations. Strive to create your story in 2,000 characters or less. This is the current character limit for a profile for LinkedIn®. Check their website to confirm current character limits or other requirements if you plan to use a version of your story on your profile. Include keywords in your summary but be careful not to intentionally overuse them in your story, summary or talking points.

You may find working from an outline useful, as well as developing different themes to help guide your story. Themes often appear after reflecting upon the questions provided throughout the workbook. Modify the process and worksheets for your individual situation and comfort level. You may not be comfortable sharing your key life events. Develop the story you will want to share with others. Then share your story with others, seek their feedback and make edits as necessary.

Opening

Your opening line should be a hook that grabs the attention of others and makes them instantly want to keep reading to learn more about you. Strive to create a single phrase with a vivid image. An example: *For me, success involves using technology to improve and save lives. I believe in the power of hard work combined with a focus on relationships and lifelong learning.* From this example, we can envision someone who takes action and is comfortable with change. What do you want others to take away from your opening line? Do you want to be known as a big picture thinker who motivates others? If so, you could develop a version of: "I believe in the power of teams. My *experience has taught me that there's nothing stronger or more productive than a diverse group of individuals who unite together to achieve a shared goal that benefits society. This type of statement can intrigue readers and make them want to learn more about you.*

Foundation

Your history serves as the foundation for your story. The foundation of your story involves your values, passions, setbacks, challenges and accomplishments. Answer the following to help create the foundation for your story.

Describe a significant life event from your childhood that impacted you.

_____

_____

_____

_____

_____

Describe a setback or challenge that impacted you as a professional.

_____

_____

_____

_____

_____

Describe a circumstance in which you were influenced by an event or individual in a workplace.

_____

_____

_____

_____

Name a professional who has influenced you since you've been in the workforce.

_____

_____

In what way did they influence you?

_____

_____

_____

_____

An example that includes history, values, passions, setbacks, challenges and accomplishments:

My experiences impressed upon me the power and importance of technology. Completing my graduate studies while working full-time, I developed the work ethic and ability to focus on value-added activities to fulfill aggressive goals. My career path in the medical devices industry has been reinforced by family illness, and I've committed my life's work to serving others.

Current Situation

Your current situation involves your knowledge, skills and abilities, talents and aspirations. Answer the questions below to help distill these elements.

Who are you now? Examples include: an experienced professional; a student; a parent; a graduate student who is also employed; a grandparent; a service member; a leader or manager; or a business owner.

_____

_____

_____

_____

What do you value?

_____

_____

_____

_____

_____

_____

Have you increased your knowledge, skills or abilities? If so, in what ways?

_____

_____

_____

_____

_____

_____

How do you add value to others in your professional role?

_____

_____

_____

_____

_____

_____

How do you add value to others in your personal life?

_____

_____

_____

_____

_____

What talents do you have? Have you developed your talents in the past few years? Do you use your talents to benefit others?

_____

_____

_____

_____

_____

_____

An example that includes knowledge, skills, abilities and talents:

I am inspired by science, my peers, and the medical devices that improve the quality and longevity of lives. To me, no greater need exists than to enable global access to life-improving and life-saving devices. I've been quite fortunate to attend one of the leading business schools in the nation for both my undergraduate and graduate studies. The first five years of my career have inspired and motivated me to acquire the knowledge and skill set to be a major contributor one day to the field. I quickly advanced from an entry-level role to assume a leadership position working under the mentorship of one of the top five scientists in the state. I've learned how to learn, and the importance of relationships to my career.

Aspirations for the Future

Your aspirations for the future involve understanding what aligns with your values, passion, talents and dreams. Reflect upon the other exercises throughout the workbook and answer the questions to help distill these elements.

What do you really aspire to do in your life? Why?

_____

_____

_____

_____

_____

_____

_____

An example that describes aspirations for the future:

My career path embodies service and lifelong learning. I'm in the zone professionally when helping advance science and discover new ways to improve the quality of life for others. I aspire to continue my quest to contribute at increased levels every year and plan to one day be one of the top leaders in my state, mentoring the next generation of young professionals entering the medical devices industry.

Consider including a closing statement and call to action if you plan to include a summary of your story on your LinkedIn® profile.

An example: *Learn more on my blog @ MaxWKelley.com (persona for illustration only).*

Story Summary Example:

For me, success involves using technology to improve and save lives. I believe in the power of hard work combined with a focus on relationships and lifelong learning.

My experiences impressed upon me the power and importance of technology. Completing my graduate studies while working full-time, I developed the work ethic and ability to focus on value-added activities to fulfill aggressive goals. My career path in the medical devices industry has been reinforced by family illness, and I've committed my life's work to serving others. I am inspired by science, my peers and the noninvasive medical devices that improve the quality and longevity of lives. To me, no greater need exists than to enable global access to life-improving and life-saving devices.

I've been quite fortunate to attend one of the leading business schools in the nation for both my undergraduate and graduate studies. The first five years of my career have inspired and motivated me to acquire the knowledge and skill set to be a major contributor one day to the field. I quickly advanced from an entry-level role to assume a leadership position working under the mentorship of one of the top five scientists in the state. I've learned how to learn and the importance of relationships to my career. My career path embodies service and lifelong learning. I'm in the zone professionally when helping advance science and discover new ways to improve the quality of life for others. I aspire to continue my quest to contribute at increased levels every year and plan to one day be one of the top scientists in my state, mentoring the next generation of young professionals entering the medical devices industry.

Learn more on my blog @ MaxWKelley.com (persona for illustration only)

Use the space provided to write your story.

_____

_____

_____

_____

_____

_____

_____

_____

_____

_____

_____

_____

_____

_____

_____

6

Understanding Your Personal Brand

Goals:

Chapter Goal:

1. Understand your personal brand's life cycle.

Reader Goal:

1. Identify the elements that I will include in my Personal Brand Development Plan.

6 Understanding Your Personal Brand

Assessing Your Personal Brand

Being active professionally on social media or being well-known in your organization for consistently adding value is great. Your brand equity grows when your efforts, messages and touch points are aligned. Others will understand you more easily if your brand equity is strong. The stronger your brand equity the better positioned you are within the market. Your efforts should strive to reinforce your core values and position you to maximize the value you add and fulfillment you receive in exchange for employment or participation. You want others to remember who you are, what you can do, and how it relates to their needs.

This Personal Brand Assessment on the next page was designed to help you understand common areas associated with personal branding. Your story, brand identity and social media presence are only three areas impacted by your efforts. This workbook focuses on these three basic areas and is not meant to be all inclusive. Advanced strategies and techniques exist and may be warranted depending upon your circumstances and goals.

Respond to the questions in the first table. Reflect upon how you responded to the assessment and decide if the questions to which you replied "no" will be areas you will include in your personal brand development plan. Then complete the second table, the Personal Brand Development Plan Decisions worksheet.

Personal Brand Assessment

Complete the Personal Brand Assessment to determine the areas in which you can better align your personal branding efforts.

YES	NO	**Your Story**
☐	☐	1. Have you identified your target audience?
☐	☐	2. Have you established your personal branding goals?
☐	☐	3. Do you have your story in written form that describes what makes you unique, reveals insight into who you are and what you value, and offers a glimpse into your career and life aspirations that is designed to provoke emotion?
☐	☐	4. Have you selected key words and message points from your story to represent you?
☐	☐	5. Have you created a pitch that describes who you are and how you add value? *Think elevator speech updated to include your potential and aspirations.*

YES	NO	**Brand Identity**
☐	☐	1. Do you use certain fonts and colors consistently across social media?
☐	☐	2. Do you have business cards?
☐	☐	3. Do you have (business style) cards to represent you independent of your employer?
☐	☐	4. Do you have a distinctive email signature?
☐	☐	5. Do you have a professional photograph (headshot)?
☐	☐	6. Do you have a website or blog?
☐	☐	7. Do you have letterhead, envelopes, labels, and presentation and memo templates?
☐	☐	8. Do you have a logo?
☐	☐	9. Do you have a tagline?
☐	☐	10. Do you have a brochure (electronic version)?

YES	NO	**Social Media**
☐	☐	1. Do you have a condensed summary of your story or message points consistently on social media (Facebook®, LinkedIn®, Twitter®, etc.?)
☐	☐	2. Do you have a fully completed profile on LinkedIn® with a professional photograph?
☐	☐	3. Do you have a professional presence on Facebook® independent of your personal Facebook® page?
☐	☐	4. Do you have a professional presence on Twitter®?
☐	☐	5. Do you have a professional presence on Aboutme.com or on other sites?

Personal Brand Development Plan Decisions

Select the areas that you will include in your Personal Brand Development Plan.

YES	NO	**Your Story**
☐	☐	1. I will identify my target audience.
☐	☐	2. I will establish personal branding goals.
☐	☐	3. I will prepare my story in written form that describes what makes me unique, reveals insight into who I am and what I value, and offers a glimpse into my career and life aspirations that is designed to provoke emotion.
☐	☐	4. I will select key words and message points from my story to represent me.
☐	☐	5. I will create a pitch that describes who I am and how I add value.
		Brand Identity
☐	☐	1. I will use certain fonts and colors consistently across social media.
☐	☐	2. I will obtain business cards.
☐	☐	3. I will obtain (business style) cards to represent me independent of my employer.
☐	☐	4. I will create a distinctive email signature.
☐	☐	5. I will obtain a professional photograph (headshot).
☐	☐	6. I will create a website or blog.
☐	☐	7. I will obtain letterhead, envelopes, labels, and presentation or memo templates.
☐	☐	8. I will obtain a logo.
☐	☐	9. I will have a tagline.
☐	☐	10. I will have a brochure (electronic version).
		Social Media
☐	☐	1. I will create a condensed summary of my story or message points and use them consistently on social media (Facebook®, LinkedIn®, Twitter®, etc.)
☐	☐	2. I will create a fully completed profile on LinkedIn® with a professional photograph.
☐	☐	3. I will have a professional presence on Facebook® independent of my personal Facebook® page.
☐	☐	4. I will have a professional presence on Twitter®.
☐	☐	5. I will have a professional presence on Aboutme.com or on other sites.

List additional elements you will include in your Personal Brand Development Plan.

_____

_____

Personal Brand Life Cycle Strategies™

The career phase you are experiencing impacts the actions you will take to develop your personal brand. Consider where you are within your personal brand life cycle to determine which strategy will position you for future success. The categories listed are merely a guide to assist with this process. You may discover that you are within two categories simultaneously, depending upon your circumstances.

Strategy	Developing Your Brand	Reinforcing Your Brand	Repositioning Your Brand	Adapting Your Brand
Objectives	Establish self within the market	Grow reputation within the market	Expand reach into additional market segments	Prepare to transition to new market segments
You as a Brand	Develop skills and abilities	Improve weaknesses and leverage strengths	Update brand messaging using innovative strategies	Leverage relationship-based tactics to offset weaknesses
Promotion	Build awareness	Provide consistent information	Identify new or updated leverage points, e.g., new accomplishments, certifications, etc.	Update knowledge, skills, and abilities as necessary
Methods	Build network	Expand network	Use multichannel tactics and technology for broad communications	Partner to maximize impact
Investment	Ensure investment is comparable with market norms	Increase investment to exceed competition	Increase or maintain investment, leverage relationships and technology to expand reach and multiply impact	Maintain investments in relationships and technology
Career Phase	Entry into the Job Market	Growth	Mature	Late Career/ Pre-retirement

Identify where you are within the Personal Brand Life Cycle Strategies™ and identify which Career Phase you are experiencing:

_____

_____

Reflect upon the:

- **_amount of time and funding_** you are willing to invest in developing, reinforcing, repositioning or adapting your personal brand; and the

- **_potential benefits and opportunity costs_** of investing your time and money in developing, reinforcing, repositioning or adapting your personal brand.

What **Strategy** will you use to develop your personal brand? Feel free to include a strategy other that what is listed:

_____

_____

_____

_____

_____

7

Understand the Competition

Goals:

Chapter Goal:

1. Understand how to conduct a competitive analysis.

Chapter Goals:

1. Identify my peers and competitors and target audience and
2. Determine how I can meet the needs of my target audience.

7 Understand the Competition

Conduct a Competitive Analysis

Your communication plans will be more effective if you have a thorough understanding of how you will position yourself in the market compared to your peers. Prior to developing your plans you should understand how others currently perceive you and how you prefer to be perceived. Then focus your efforts on communicating the attributes you want to be known for, while highlighting the ways in which you can add value.

Next, decide if you will develop your personal brand to emphasize how you add value in your current position or if you want to develop your personal brand for a job or career transition. You may want to position yourself for advancement from your current position or you may be preparing to transition into the marketplace from an educational or training program with limited professional experience. Your plans may involve transitioning from your current position to a new position with a different organization. If you seek to change jobs, do your research and understand the industry you want to work in; its history, market drivers and anticipated growth and changes in addition to understanding the level at which you want to work.

> "Your communication plans will be more effective if you have a thorough understanding of how you will position yourself in the market compared to your peers."

A competitive analysis can give you a better understanding of current in-person and online communication techniques used in professional social environments. The value of "netiquette" and the use of technology and social norms should not be underestimated—they are expected and powerful. If you are not up to date with current practices you may not be offered opportunities to participate or even be employed. Completing a competitive analysis will help you think in terms of how you can meet the needs of the market instead of simply attempting to promote what you have to offer. Remember, the "market" I'm referring to is really defined by you and consists of who you want to reach.

A competitive analysis can also give you an idea of what employers and recruiters experience when they interact with others. Conduct a competitive analysis prior to finalizing the positioning for your personal brand. Discovering how others position themselves can help you better understand how your story and compelling value proposition can be used to differentiate you within the marketplace. Job search sites such as Indeed.com® and others offer the option of placing a viewable resume online. Oftentimes you can view resumes on these websites and gain a better understanding of how others present and position themselves.

To begin your competitive analysis: 1) *identify* your competitors or peers; 2) *describe* your competitors or peers; and 3) *understand* how your competitors or peers are presenting themselves in the marketplace. Next, *acknowledge* who you intend to reach with your messaging and engagement: 4) *identify* your target audience; 5) *describe* your target audience; 6) *understand* your target audiences' needs; 7) *summarize* how you can meet those needs; and 8) *identify* any gaps between your target audience needs and what you have to offer.

Competitive Analysis

Step 1: *Identify* your competitors or peers

Who do you consider three of your competitors or peers? You may or may not know these individuals. Identify individuals who could compete with you for a job or other opportunity. This workbook is as confidential as you keep it, so help yourself by being honest. You may discover that a very close colleague or friend would be a very strong competitor of yours if both of you were to apply for the same position. For the sake of completing the exercise, use pseudonyms for the actual individuals if this makes you feel more comfortable—the purpose here is for you to identify five individuals that you could consider your competitors or peers.

Competitor or Peer One

Name:

_____

Competitor or Peer Two

Name:

_____

Competitor or Peer Three

Name:

_____

Competitor or Peer Four

Name:

_____

Competitor or Peer Five

Name:

_____

Step 2: *Describe* your competitors or peers

Include attributes, achievements or categories that describe your competitors or peers. For example:

Example One: *Alicia received three promotions in the past eight years while completing a graduate program and being recognized for community service.*

Example Two: *Ryan has been named volunteer of the year by his employer, a leading pharmaceutical company, and selected for their internal leadership rotational program that provides international and management experiences.*

_____

_____

_____

_____

_____

Step 3: *Understand* how your competitors or peers present themselves

This step involves identifying five of your competitors or peers and identifying how they present themselves and engage with others. You should strive to understand how they are unique and the ways in which they stand out. What you discover may surprise you. Yes, some of the individuals you review may have figured out which marketing tactics help them stand out or how they can provide a consistent professional impression. The truly impressive individuals are often those that add value to others. How they do this makes them unique and helps differentiate them from others. They may share information that's important to others or information that evokes emotion and resonates with others. Much continues to be said about using storytelling to connect with audiences. Telling your story can help you connect with others, and when shared with authenticity and goodwill you can establish trust and strengthen relationships over time. When this occurs, telling your story serves to build a foundation from which you can accentuate how you communicate and connect with others.

Select five of your peers or competitors and identify:

Do they use social media? If so, what social media sites do they use? LinkedIn®, Facebook®, Twitter®, Google+® or others?

Competitor or Peer One _____

_____

Competitor or Peer Two _____

_____

Competitor or Peer Three _____

_____

Competitor or Peer Four _____

_____

Competitor or Peer Five _____

_____

Do they participate in two-way conversations with others? If so, to what extent? Are they:

- an infrequent user (seldom engaged, quarterly or less);
- an active user (engaged weekly); or
- a very active user (engaged daily)?

Competitor or Peer One _____

_____

Competitor or Peer Two _____

_____

Competitor or Peer Three _____

_____

Competitor or Peer Four _____

_____

Competitor or Peer Five _____

_____

Do your competitors or peers use social media to send messages without engaging?

Competitor or Peer One _____

_____

Competitor or Peer Two _____

_____

Competitor or Peer Three _____

_____

Competitor or Peer Four _____

_____

Competitor or Peer Five _____

_____

Do they mix personal and professional messaging?

Competitor or Peer One _____

_____

Competitor or Peer Two _____

_____

Competitor or Peer Three _____

_____

Competitor or Peer Four _____

_____

Competitor or Peer Five _____

_____

Consider the following to improve your understanding of where your competitors and peers invest their time and efforts. Circle all that apply and add others.

Social Media	LinkedIn®/Other Groups	Volunteering
Indeed.com®/Other Job Search Sites	Alumni/Other College Sites	Boards
Professional Associations	Games/Interests/Hobbies	Sports
Blogs	Continuing Education	Google® Search and Alerts
Churches	In-Person Networking Groups	Activism

Identify three ways in which you have seen your competitors or peers use social media or in-person networking that you will consider adopting.

1. _____

2. _____

3. _____

Examples:

1. *Engaging in conversations on LinkedIn®*

2. *Starting a local networking group*

3. *Participating in Google+® hangouts*

Step 4: *Identify* your target audience

Consider both your current target audience and potential future audience when you create your personal brand development plan. Anticipating future audiences can be challenging because it involves evaluating a variety of factors and making your best guess of what industry you will work in and your functional role within it. Identifying your target audience needs is significant in this step. It is important to remember that developing your personal brand effectively involves communicating to add value to others. This involves anticipating the needs of others and looking beyond the messages you simply want them to receive. An example of this could involve a mid-level early career information technology (IT) professional who seeks a promotion to a role within another related but different industry (e.g., IT healthcare professional seeking to transition to a biotech start-up). In this example the professional would most likely need to develop a broad strategy that involves researching to identify audience needs and then developing engagement and communications plans to help others understand how they could add value within a new industry.

Who is your target audience?

_____

_____

_____

_____

Step 5: *Describe* your target audience

Use the following questions to create a description of your target audience:

1. What are the responsibilities, values, interests and goals of your target audience?

_____

_____

_____

_____

2. Where is your target audience engaged online and in person?

_____

_____

_____

_____

3. When does your target audience engage online and in person?

_____

_____

_____

4. Why does your target audience engage online and in person?

_____

_____

_____

5. Who does your target audience engage with online and in person?

_____

_____

_____

6. How does your target audience engage online and in person?

_____

_____

_____

Step 6: *Understand* your target audiences' needs

Once you have determined your target audience and identified their role, responsibilities, values and interests you can identify and understand their needs. Remember that your level of understanding may be influenced by your goals and the role you seek to assume. You may seek to be an employee, colleague, volunteer or mentor to the members of your target audience. For example, if your audience consists of professionals within an association in which you just became a member, you could begin by networking in person to discover current topics, trends and shared pain points among members and the leadership. This could be followed-up by joining affinity groups, identifying alumni or other shared interests as well as participating in online networking and learning opportunities. The objective is to understand what purpose you can serve for your target audience. This helps you know where to invest your time. You may find it useful to organize your target audience needs for future reference and planning.

Use the space provided to list your target audience's needs.

_____

_____

_____

Step 7: *Summarize* how you can meet those needs

One area which I have seen underutilized involves individuals being bridges to one another. Many are of the belief that they must obtain direct access to the person in charge or the individual who is the gatekeeper to the person in charge. Depending upon your goals this may be true, but I encourage you to consider the value of recommendations and the extent to which you can use them to enrich relationships and to progress in your career. Use the following space to summarize your target audience's needs and how you can meet their needs.

_____

_____

_____

Let's continue with the previous example. In this situation, your audience may include professionals in the association that you just joined. You've learned a great deal about the professionals and their needs through networking and affinity groups. From your interactions with them you have identified that they are challenged by a lack of time to volunteer in their community due to work and family obligations. They are also experiencing a lack of employer-sponsored professional development opportunities resulting in their feeling unappreciated and stuck in their current positions without the possibility for growth or promotion. These are the group's main shared pain points.

You understand that your time management skills, interpersonal abilities, creativity and resource management may position you to add value to this group. You learned excellent time management tactics during your studies, and in your role as a community liaison you developed programs that were beneficial for both communities and organizations. Both of these experiences position you to transfer these skills to a different context and add value to the association members while further developing your personal brand. In this situation your summary could include:

- Suggest the formation of a work/life balance affinity group where you could further explore the time management challenges of the group and serve as a facilitator to develop programming to share time management techniques that could be adapted for group members.

- Explore the possibilities of job rotations, expanded job duties for limited periods of time, or grassroots learning initiatives that involve members of the group providing training at each other's organizations during lunch periods or after work.

Step 8: *Identify* any gaps between your target audience needs and what you have to offer

Determine what could prevent you from meeting the needs of your target audience. Your input could be rebuffed due to internal politics or leadership priorities that you failed to identify. You could also encounter resistance due to competing priorities. Other affinity groups, teams or individuals may already be tasked with planning programs for the association. The gaps in the audience needs you have identified and what you have to offer may involve:

- your longevity with the group;
- a lack of understanding of the group norms and culture; and
- a lack of communication with leadership.

Test your assumptions by spending more time learning about the organization and its goals and leadership once you have identified what you believe may hinder your effectiveness. Inquire about the possibility of an in-depth orientation, on-boarding process or mentor opportunities that could help you eliminate the gaps between your target audience needs and what you have to offer. Use the space provided to identify any gaps between your target audience's needs and what you offer.

_____

_____

_____

_____

_____

_____

_____

_____

_____

_____

_____

_____

_____

_____

_____

_____

_____

_____

_____

8

Create Your Personal Brand Development Plan

Goals:

Chapter Goal:

1. Guide the creation of a personal brand development plan using examples and templates.

Reader Goal:

1. Set goals and create the foundation for my personal brand development plan.

8 Create Your Personal Brand Development Plan

Your personal brand development plan involves envisioning your future and assessing your current situation, assets and challenges and creating a practical plan to achieve your vision. You already own one of the most important elements critical to your success—it's your story. Up to this point you may not have considered it an asset or thought how it can connect you with others. Your story can evoke emotion in others and help them appreciate you in a variety of ways. Your brand identity already exists as well. You may simply decide to refine it to reflect your envisioned future instead of maintaining it to reflect your past accomplishments and current state. Social media can be a differentiator and help distinguish you from your peers. Individuals who share information or connect others become known for adding value. Social media enables this instantaneously and those who are connected in real time have a tendency to stay relevant and engaged. Complete the exercises in this section to begin creating your personal brand development plan.

The figure on the next page depicts the basic elements involved in developing a personal brand.

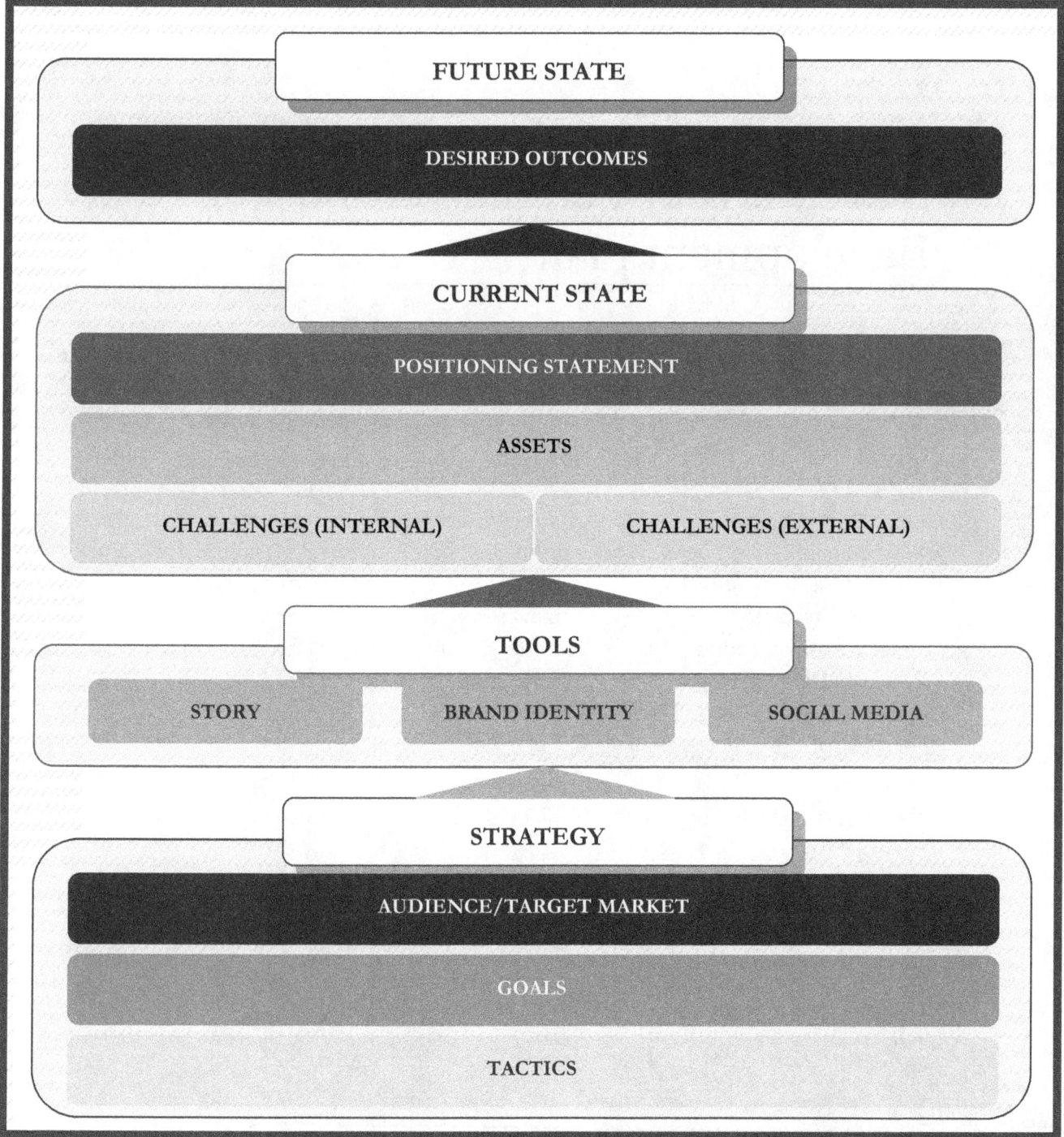

FUTURE STATE

DESIRED OUTCOMES

CURRENT STATE

POSITIONING STATEMENT

ASSETS

CHALLENGES (INTERNAL)	CHALLENGES (EXTERNAL)

TOOLS

STORY	BRAND IDENTITY	SOCIAL MEDIA

STRATEGY

AUDIENCE/TARGET MARKET

GOALS

TACTICS

Take a moment to reflect on your ideal future state. What do you want your career and your life to look like one year, five years, or ten years from now? What do you want people to think of you?

_____

_____

_____

_____

_____

_____

_____

_____

_____

_____

_____

_____

_____

_____

Review the example table, Developing Your Personal Brand, on the next page. Then use the notes you made above to fill in the Developing Your Personal Brand template.

Developing Your Personal Brand Example

FUTURE STATE		

DESIRED OUTCOMES:

- Mentorship success stories
- Peer group engaged
- Service learning program participation

POSITIONING STATEMENT	ASSETS	CHALLENGES
To be a value-added source for others by leveraging my talents and network in service as a mentor and leader while growing my thought leadership and brand equity.	<ul><li>Professional summary developed based upon my story</li><li>Depth of expertise within a niche specialization</li><li>Importance of this niche specialization to the market</li><li>Medium-sized, engaged network</li></ul>	*INTERNAL* <ul><li>Concept of personal branding is new to me</li><li>Time (already overcommitted)</li><li>Lack of consistent messages on social media</li><li>Personal branding activities tactical, not strategic or connected</li><li>Desired personal branding position not defined in measurable terms</li></ul> *EXTERNAL* <ul><li>Competition in job market (need to stay current with job market and service learning practices)</li><li>Local networking opportunities</li><li>Lack of network diversity</li><li>Strategy and diversity of mentors</li></ul>
AUDIENCE/TARGET MARKET **Peers**<ul><li>Inspire service</li><li>Build and leverage network</li></ul>**Corporations**<ul><li>Thought leadership</li><li>Volunteer coordination of service learning programs</li></ul>	**GOALS**<ul><li>Grow thought leadership reach</li><li>Elevate brand awareness regionally</li><li>Design and implement a personal brand development plan</li><li>Enrich existing relationships and increase breadth of my network</li></ul>	**TACTICS**<ul><li>Update my brand identity</li><li>Refine value proposition, messaging and elevator pitch</li><li>Create messaging action plans for targeted individuals</li><li>Create brand development plan with timeline</li><li>Identify appropriate benchmarks</li></ul>

Developing Your Personal Brand Template

FUTURE STATE

DESIRED OUTCOMES:

_____

_____

_____

CURRENT STATE		
POSITIONING STATEMENT	**ASSETS**	**CHALLENGES**
		INTERNAL
		EXTERNAL

STRATEGY		
AUDIENCE/TARGET MARKET	**GOALS**	**TACTICS**

Goal Setting for Competitive Advantage

Goal setting can help prevent the unnecessary loss of time and money by encouraging you to decide what resources you will need to accomplish your goals. Goals are accomplishments to be achieved. They provide direction and can be quite motivational. The SMART Goal Setting Method is a classic goal setting method. It represents goals that are Specific, Measurable, Achievable, Realistic and Time-bound. You may be familiar with the SMART Goal Setting Method, but today I am introducing you to the SMARTER™ Goal Setting Method. You can surpass the impact typically realized from using the traditional SMART Goal Setting Method when you use the SMARTER™ Goal Setting Method. This is due to an emphasis on multiplying the ***effort expended*** combined with a ***focus on relationships***—no longer is simply going from point A to point B the key—how you go about getting to point B can make a difference in impact and in time and money saved. Review the examples to gain an understanding of this method.

SMART Goal Setting Example

GOAL	OBJECTIVES	STRATEGIES	TACTICS		
Accomplishment to be achieved.	Specific, measurable steps that have a completion date.	The "thinking" aspect involved in achieving your objectives.	The "doing" aspect involved in achieving a strategy.		
EXAMPLE					
Increase my online professional network.	Increase my LinkedIn® connections to 250 by 1 March.	Use research and Internet marketing activities to create a plan for increasing my online network using social media.	Update resume, biography and compelling value proposition.		

SMARTER™ Goal Setting Example

GOAL	OBJECTIVES	STRATEGIES	TACTICS	EFFORT EXPENDED	FOCUS ON RELATIONSHIPS
Accomplishment to be achieved.	Specific, measurable steps that have a completion date.	The "thinking" aspect involved in achieving your objectives.	The "doing" aspect involved in achieving a strategy.	Amount and quality of effort put forth.	Frequency and richness of engagement.
EXAMPLE					
Increase my online professional network.	Increase my LinkedIn® connections to 250 by 1 March.	Use research and Internet marketing activities to create a plan for increasing my online network using social media.	Update resume, biography and compelling value proposition.	<u>Option</u>: Update LinkedIn® profile, maintaining same style of verbiage and formatting. <u>Option</u>: Research and identify current practices and determine if appropriate.	Join Groups and engage on a regular basis (weekly) by asking and answering questions and adding value for others.

Career Goals Example

GOAL	OBJECTIVES	STRATEGIES	TACTICS	EFFORT EXPENDED	FOCUS ON RELATIONSHIPS
Accomplishment to be achieved.	Specific, measurable steps that have a completion date.	The "thinking" aspect involved in achieving your objectives.	The "doing" aspect involved in achieving a strategy.	Amount and quality of effort put forth.	Frequency and richness of engagement.
CAREER GOALS					
Be assigned responsibility for a $5M project/initiative.	Discuss with VP by 1 Feb.	Identify a dormant initiative that has been tabled due to a lack of resources or management.	Review annual reports and departmental and organizational strategic plans for the past three years.	Work on research and report preparation before and after normal work day.	Seek input from peers and management.
Join a Board of Advisors at my Alma Mater.	Meet with the Department Chair by 1 March.	Conceptualize approach for industry analysis.	Develop an industry analysis and include current market drivers, employment forecasts by graduate type and profile the top 10 corporations.	Work on documentation before and after normal work day and during lunch meetings to gather information and validate assumptions.	Seek feedback from industry and academic leaders, peers and management.
Be selected for senior level career path.	Express an interest in being selected for advancement to Assoc. VP by 1 April.	Identify a minimum of three examples from the past three years that evidence my abilities and willingness to work at a higher level.	Document the money made or saved from the three examples from the past three years and include the impact on the organization.	Work on documentation before and after normal work day.	Seek recommendations from peers and upper level management regarding my performance.
Be elected an officer in the Medical Devices Industry Forum.	Meet with Forum leadership by 1 May.	Conceptualize platform for leadership role.	Create a one page leadership statement.	Work on documentation before and after normal work day.	Seek feedback from Forum members, peers and management.
Be promoted from Ex. Director to Assoc. VP.	Discuss career path, opportunities for advancement and stretch assignments with my VP by 1 July.	Map out potential money saving initiatives and ways to increase revenue and decrease costs.	Research, document and prioritize money-saving initiatives and ways to increase revenue and decrease costs.	Work on research and report preparation before and after normal work day.	Solicit input from peers in and outside the organization and cite them in the report.

Career Goals Template

Use the following template to list your goals.

GOAL	OBJECTIVES	STRATEGIES	TACTICS	EFFORT EXPENDED	FOCUS ON RELATIONSHIPS
Accomplishment to be achieved.	Specific, measurable steps that have a completion date.	The "thinking" aspect involved in achieving your objectives.	The "doing" aspect involved in achieving a strategy.	Amount and quality of effort put forth.	Frequency and richness of engagement.
CURRENT CAREER GOALS					

Your Story Example

GOAL	OBJECTIVES	STRATEGIES	TACTICS	EFFORT EXPENDED	FOCUS ON RELATIONSHIPS
Accomplishment to be achieved.	Specific, measurable steps that have a completion date.	The "thinking" aspect involved in achieving your objectives.	The "doing" aspect involved in achieving a strategy.	Amount and quality of effort put forth.	Frequency and richness of engagement.
YOUR STORY					
Write my story to reflect my knowledge, skills, abilities, values, passions, accomplishments, setbacks, interests and aspirations.	Complete a draft of my story by 1 March.	Reflect upon my answers to the exercises in this workbook and decide how I want to position myself in the market short and long term.	Complete the exercises in this workbook.	Work on the exercises in the workbook before and after work and on the weekends.	Seek feedback from my wife after I complete each section of exercises.
Refine my story and prepare it for distribution.	Complete my story by 1 May.	Decide who I will seek input from, ensuring a well-rounded representation from my past, present and anticipated future.	Create a schedule of who I will talk with weekly, and work from that schedule until I have spoken with everyone.	Gather feedback after work, on the weekends and during lunches.	Seek feedback from those who have supported my development as well as those that I've received constructive criticism from in the past.
Use my story to create a positioning statement, elevator pitch and talking points.	Complete a positioning statement, elevator pitch and talking points by 15 May.	Reflect upon the various audiences that I will target and think about their needs, attributes and experiences.	Create personas for my target audiences and then create the positioning statement, elevator pitch and talking points.	Work on the personas, positioning statement, elevator pitch and talking points before and after work and on the weekends.	Seek feedback from my wife and peers and refine as needed.
Use my story and evaluate its effectiveness.	Use my story in my social media profiles online from 1 June to 1 Sept.	Think about the ways in which I can determine if I'm making progress toward my goals.	Create milestones and outcomes to guide and measure my performance.	Work on the milestones and outcomes before and after work and on the weekends.	Seek feedback from my peers and refine as needed.
Update my story bi-annually and as needed.	Update my story in January and June annually.	Reflect upon the ways in which I may be changing and how these changes impact my story.	Keep a journal to briefly note changes in my knowledge, skills, abilities, values, passions, accomplishments, setbacks, interests and aspirations.	Makes notes in my journal nightly.	Discuss changes with my wife monthly.

Your Story Template

The next three templates are to be used for your personal branding goals related to your story, brand identity and social media. Use the assessment you previously completed and the examples to assist you in this process.

GOAL	OBJECTIVES	STRATEGIES	TACTICS	EFFORT EXPENDED	FOCUS ON RELATIONSHIPS
Accomplishment to be achieved.	Specific, measurable steps that have a completion date.	The "thinking" aspect involved in achieving your objectives.	The "doing" aspect involved in achieving a strategy.	Amount and quality of effort put forth.	Frequency and richness of engagement.
YOUR STORY					

Your Brand Identity Example

GOAL	OBJECTIVES	STRATEGIES	TACTICS	EFFORT EXPENDED	FOCUS ON RELATIONSHIPS
Accomplishment to be achieved.	Specific, measurable steps that have a completion date.	The "thinking" aspect involved in achieving your objectives.	The "doing" aspect involved in achieving a strategy.	Amount and quality of effort put forth.	Frequency and richness of engagement.
YOUR BRAND IDENTITY					
Use professional photographs on my social media profiles, blog, association profile and for presentations and articles.	Obtain professional photographs by 1 March.	Reflect upon the best professional photographs I've seen during the past year.	Research samples and the photographers who took the photographs; obtain quotes and select a photographer and wardrobe.	Research before and after work and on the weekends.	Share the rationale for my personal branding plan briefly with everyone that I contact to request photographer information
Use select fonts and colors to represent my brand.	Select fonts and colors by 1 March.	Decide what characteristics I want my fonts to represent and what emotions I want to evoke with color.	Research colors and fonts to understand what they represent and communicate.	Research before and after work and on the weekends.	Solicit input from a graphic designer and feedback from my wife and peers regarding my options and preferences.
Use select letterhead, envelopes, note cards, labels, business cards (independent of my employer) and a presentation template to represent my personal brand.	Obtain branded letterhead, envelopes, note cards, labels, business cards (independent of my employer) and a presentation template by 1 April.	Decide what emotions I want to evoke and what style I want to present.	Research stationary, business card trends, and use the information gathered regarding fonts and colors.	Research before and after work, at lunch and on the weekends.	Solicit input from a graphic designer and feedback from my wife and peers regarding my options and preferences.
Use a branded email signature, logo and brochure to represent my personal brand.	Obtain a branded email signature, logo and brochure by 1 April.	Decide what I want to communicate, emotions I want to evoke, and what style I want to present.	Work with a freelance marketing consultant.	Connect as needed and draft copy and review feedback before and after work, at lunch and on the weekends.	Solicit input from a graphic designer and feedback from my wife and peers regarding my options and preferences.
Use a branded blog to establish my thought leadership and build my brand equity.	Launch my blog by 1 May.	Decide what I want to communicate, which emotions I want to evoke and what style I want to present.	Work with a web site design firm.	Connect as needed and draft copy and review feedback before and after work, at lunch and on the weekends.	Solicit feedback from my wife and peers and revise as necessary.

Your Brand Identity Template

GOAL	OBJECTIVES	STRATEGIES	TACTICS	EFFORT EXPENDED	FOCUS ON RELATIONSHIPS
Accomplishment to be achieved.	Specific, measurable steps that have a completion date.	The "thinking" aspect involved in achieving your objectives.	The "doing" aspect involved in achieving a strategy.	Amount and quality of effort put forth.	Frequency and richness of engagement.
YOUR BRAND IDENTITY					

Social Media and Online Presence Example

GOAL	OBJECTIVES	STRATEGIES	TACTICS	EFFORT EXPENDED	FOCUS ON RELATIONSHIPS
Accomplishment to be achieved.	Specific, measurable steps that have a completion date.	The "thinking" aspect involved in achieving your objectives.	The "doing" aspect involved in achieving a strategy.	Amount and quality of effort put forth.	Frequency and richness of engagement.
SOCIAL MEDIA AND ONLINE PRESENCE					
Understand my social media presence.	Audit my current social media presence by 1 March.	Reflect upon and determine the value I've added through social media.	Create a list of the social media sites I use and rank my use according to frequency and the richness of the engagement (e.g., one-way, two-way or group).	Compile information before and after work and on the weekends.	Discuss with my peers.
Establish professional presence on LinkedIn®, Facebook®, Twitter® and Google+®.	Create profiles on LinkedIn®, Facebook®, Twitter® and Google+® by 1 April.	Decide which social media sites are the most appropriate for me.	Read books, norms and setup guides and create profiles with consist content on each site.	Compile information before and after work and on the weekends.	Seek input from my peers and others on social media regarding best practices.
Have an engaged, robust and diverse network on a variety of social media sites.	Invite peers and other professionals to connect with me by 1 May.	Determine which groups and organizations I want to associate with my personal brand.	Create a list of individuals from my past and current situation I'd like to engage with on social media.	Compile information before and after work and on the weekends.	Seek input from my peers and others on social media regarding best practices.
			Create an engagement plan with a timeline that forecasts a certain amount of time be dedicated to social media.		
			Create plans to measure my effectiveness according to a periodic timeline.		

Social Media and Online Presence Template

GOAL	OBJECTIVES	STRATEGIES	TACTICS	EFFORT EXPENDED	FOCUS ON RELATIONSHIPS
Accomplishment to be achieved.	Specific, measurable steps that have a completion date.	The "thinking" aspect involved in achieving your objectives.	The "doing" aspect involved in achieving a strategy.	Amount and quality of effort put forth.	Frequency and richness of engagement.
SOCIAL MEDIA AND ONLINE PRESENCE					

9

Network to Strengthen Your Brand

Goals:

Chapter Goal:

1. Demonstrate how to create a strategic networking plan.

Reader Goal:

1. Use the examples and templates to create a strategic networking plan.

9 Network to Strengthen Your Brand

Do you have a network of professionals who know you for your ability to use your skills in a variety of roles across industries? Remember it's not just who you know—it's who knows you and what you're capable of. Would they avoid letting you go if cutbacks were to occur at your company? Are you someone who does a "good" job but isn't well known? Can you really afford not to position yourself for being known for the work you've done **and** for the work you're capable of?

Passive networking, e.g., linking up online via a social network or exchanging business cards with someone and seldom talking with them will most likely not lead to opportunities or a successful job search. More importantly, such methods should not be relied upon to produce the results you want. It's critical that you develop a variety of networks. You must also give in order to receive and be willing to connect others and offer support if possible. You never know when someone you have helped may be in a position to help you. Use the following to develop a targeted networking strategy and locate others who are connected to decision makers. While the following depicts how to connect for the purpose of securing employment it can also be used to network strategically to build your brand equity.

Planning to Network

Step One: Identify Organizations

The first step in effectively networking for a new opportunity or career is to acknowledge where you want to work and why. While some individuals just "want a job" others prefer to seek a career in which they can flourish at a different level. Securing this type of position often begins with knowing yourself, which involves understanding your passions and preferences as well as your knowledge, skills and abilities. Several options exist to help you identify organizations where you may prefer to work, including a list of employers by state and a list of public and private companies worldwide.

Step Two: Identify Targets

Once you have identified an organization in which you may want to work, write down who you want to connect with within the organization. This may be an operational or human resources manager or perhaps a vice president.

Step Three: Identify Direct Connections

Next, write down who you know within the organization and reflect upon how well you know them. Who are they connected to within the organization? Are they connected to the individuals you ultimately seek to connect with? Are they in a position to support your applying for a vacancy, or could they provide insight about future vacancies? Consider these individuals *direct connections* in your network—they can directly connect you to your preferred place of employment.

Step Four: Identify Bridges

Perhaps you lack any direct connections to your preferred place of employment. Identify who in your network is connected to anyone at your preferred place of employment and plan to engage with them. Consider these individuals *bridges* in your network. Try professional and personal connections and online professional networking tools such as LinkedIn® if you lack direct knowledge of who may be a bridge.

Step Five: Identify Alternate Bridges or Connections

Lastly, if you lack direct connections or bridges, focus on who you need to connect with at the organization. This may be a hiring manager, vice president or divisional director, manager or supervisor. For the sake of creating a strategic networking plan consider them your "target". An advanced Google® search may prove useful to you in this instance, or you may be able to obtain this information via the organization's website, from a professional association or via a local chamber of commerce. Remember to consider the colleagues of your friends and family, your alumni associations and local community members as potential connections and bridges. Once you have located groups or activities these individuals participate in, you can consider connecting with them via someone in the group or by joining the group yourself if it's of interest to you.

Numerous resources are available online related to networking. You may discover that your obligations permit more active networking at some times than at others and that's understandable. What's important is that you consistently focus on staying engaged with your network and not simply focused on increasing the number of contacts you have—*it's quality, not quantity that matters*. Your professional success depends in large part on networking. Remember online networking is important, but perhaps more important is establishing and growing relationships in person.

PLANNING TO NETWORK: INSIGHT					
Organizations	Targets (Who You Seek to Meet)	Direct Connections (Your Contacts)	Bridges (Individuals Who Are Connected to Your Target)	Alternate Bridges or Connections	Insight (What is the connection?)
Becton Dickinson	Bill Jones, VP Planning Becton Dickinson	Alexander Smith, Indiana University Alumnus			Our children go to the same school
Smiths Medical	Sally Myers, Director Operations, Smiths Medical		Jill Weaver		We serve on the same United Way Committee
Cook Medical	Jan Fleming, Director of Manufacturing		Ross Townsend, Saint Mary-of-the-Woods College Alumnus		He went through the Master of Leadership Development program with my wife

Fictitious names listed above for illustration purposes

PLANNING TO NETWORK: OBJECTIVES					
Organizations	**Targets** (Who You Seek to Meet)	**Direct Connections** (Your Contacts)	**Bridges** (Individuals Who Are Connected to Your Target)	**Alternate Bridges or Connections**	**Objectives** (What do you want to do/learn?)
Becton Dickinson	Bill Jones, VP Planning Becton Dickinson	Alexander Smith, Indiana University Alumnus			Industry insight
Smiths Medical	Sally Myers, Director Operations, Smiths Medical		Jill Weaver		Introduction
Cook Medical	Jan Fleming, Director of Manufacturing		Ross Townsend, Saint Mary-of-the-Woods College Alumnus		Introduction

Fictitious names listed above for illustration purposes

SAMPLE NETWORKING PLAN				
Who You Will Connect With (Could be a direct connection, bridge or target)	**How You Will Connect**	**When You Will Connect**	**Date Connection Made**	**Next Steps**
Alexander Smith, Indiana University Alumnus	Via the Indiana University LinkedIn® Alumni Group. Personalize an invitation to connect and point out that in addition to both of you being IU Alumni; you understand your children go to the same school.	This week		Once connected, thank him for connecting and offer to put your network at his disposal should he be interested in connecting with anyone. After he responds, ask if he'd be willing to join you in a brief phone conversation.
Jill Weaver	In person or if you're unable to connect in person send an email. Don't wait until the next United Way meeting.	Prior to or after the next the United Way meeting ask if she'd be interested in joining you for coffee/lunch.		Schedule the coffee/lunch. Afterward, thank her for meeting you.
Jan Fleming	Ross Townsend introduces us via email.	Next week		Schedule a coffee/lunch meeting.

Fictitious names listed above for illustration purposes

Planning Templates

Use the following templates to develop your networking plan.

PLANNING TO NETWORK: INSIGHT					
Organizations	Targets (Who You Seek to Meet)	Direct Connections (Your Contacts)	Bridges (Individuals Who Are Connected to Your Target)	Alternate Bridges or Connections	Insight (What is the connection?)

| PLANNING TO NETWORK: OBJECTIVES | | | | | |
Organizations	Targets (Who You Seek to Meet)	Direct Connections (Your Contacts)	Bridges (Individuals Who Are Connected to Your Target)	Alternate Bridges or Connections	Objectives (What do you want to do/learn?)

NETWORKING PLAN				
Who You Will Connect With (Could be a direct connection, bridge or target)	**How You Will Connect**	**When You Will Connect**	**Date Connection Made**	**Next Steps**

10

Measure Your Progress and Celebrate Success

Goals:

Chapter Goal:

1. Raise awareness of the importance of measuring progress and celebrating success.

Reader Goal:

1. Determine how I will measure progress and celebrate success.

10 Measure Your Progress and Celebrate Success

Let's assume you have completed the self-assessments; identified your knowledge, skills, abilities and passions; written your story; completed a competitive analysis; and drafted networking, brand identity, social media and networking plans. You then used these to create your personal brand development plan that includes goals with deadlines. Fantastic! Remember to periodically review your progress and celebrate your success. Many professionals find this helps motivate them to continue working on their goals. Take time to review your circumstances if at any point you become discouraged or even overwhelmed by the amount of activities you're attempting to pursue in addition to your regular work load and personal obligations. On occasion you may discover that the best action for you involves not taking any action. Deciding not to pursue a goal can be best for you depending upon your circumstances. Each of us has a limited amount of time and resources and we have to decide what we will pursue given a variety of factors including opportunity costs. Factor in opportunity costs and keep in mind if you choose to pursue Goal A instead of Goal B you are losing the value you would have received if you would have pursued Goal B. The process does not need to be overly complicated, but be sure you consider the elements appropriate for your situation.

> "Having a fulfilling professional life should involve accomplishing goals that you've set and celebrating in ways appropriate for and appreciated by you."

The outcomes for your goals should be apparent. When this is the case it is easy to identify if you have achieved your goals. On occasion our goals are closely related to one another. Success in one goal sometimes also involves success in another. For example, accomplishing your networking goals could help you realize both professional development and career goals. Progress in one area may help you make progress in another. Other ways in which you can measure your progress involves identifying your social media scores using online providers. I wouldn't become overly concerned with striving for a certain set of numbers unless you seek a position in which this is a requirement. I suggest focusing on quality rather than quantity. You can also obtain feedback from your network, family and friends. Those closest to you will often know the extent to which you're changing your behavior or working toward your goals. The performance of your direct reports can also be a sign of your performance. You can also analyze your performance working with both individuals and teams. Performing a personal brand or social media audit can also provide you with valuable information. Other measures may include customer acquisition, sales and retention.

Celebrating success should come naturally for us but it can be overlooked quickly and completely. Just as you define what success means, you should also decide how you will celebrate or at the very least decide that you will celebrate. You may find you want to celebrate with friends, family and supporters at different times and in different ways. What's important is remembering to celebrate and give yourself credit for what you have achieved. This is important, because you don't want to burn yourself out or tire or frustrate yourself from constantly striving to realize your goals. Having a fulfilling professional life should involve accomplishing goals that you've set and celebrating in ways appropriate for and appreciated by you. Personal preferences, styles and resources naturally factor in to our decisions. Reward yourself for all of the initiative you've shown, your hard work and the results you've realized. Remember to update your supporters on your progress. Professionals who serve as both mentors and mentees can appreciate the success of others and the rewards of helping others. Appreciate and celebrate those who empower your success.

Appendices

A

Personal Brand
Development Plan Example

Connect To Serve

MAX W. KELLEY PERSONAL BRAND DEVELOPMENT PLAN
2014

Table of Contents

Executive Summary

Persona used in the example is Max W. Kelley, second year MBA student taking courses via distance while working full-time. Max has five years of professional work experience in the medical devices industry.

Story Summary

For me, success involves using technology to improve and save lives. I believe in the power of hard work combined with a focus on relationships and lifelong learning.

My experiences impressed upon me the power and importance of technology. Completing my graduate studies while working full-time, I developed the work ethic and ability to focus on value-added activities to fulfill aggressive goals. My career path in the medical devices industry has been reinforced by family illness, and I've committed my life's work to serving others. I am inspired by science, my peers and the noninvasive medical devices that improve the quality and longevity of lives. To me, no greater need exists than to enable global access to life-improving and life-saving devices.

I've been quite fortunate to attend one of the leading business schools in the nation for both my undergraduate and graduate studies. The first five years of my career have inspired and motivated me to acquire the knowledge and skill set to be a major contributor, one day, to the field. I quickly advanced from an entry level role to assume a leadership position working under the mentorship of one of the top five scientists in the state. I've learned how to learn, and the importance of relationships to my career. My career path embodies service and lifelong learning. I'm in the zone professionally when helping advance science and discover new ways to improve the quality of life for others. I aspire to continue my quest to contribute at increased levels every year, and plan to one day be one of the top scientists in my state, mentoring the next generation of young professionals entering the medical devices industry.

Learn more on my blog @ MaxWKelley.com (persona for illustration only)

Career Goals

GOAL	OBJECTIVES	STRATEGIES	TACTICS	EFFORT EXPENDED	FOCUS ON RELATIONSHIPS
Accomplishment to be achieved.	Specific, measurable steps that have a completion date.	The "thinking" aspect involved in achieving your objectives.	The "doing" aspect involved in achieving a strategy.	Amount and quality of effort put forth.	Frequency and richness of engagement.
CAREER GOALS					
Be assigned responsibility for a $5M project/initiative.	Discuss with VP by 1 Feb.	Identify a dormant initiative that has been tabled due to a lack of resources or management.	Review annual reports and departmental and organizational strategic plans for the past three years.	Work on research and report preparation before and after normal work day.	Seek input from peers and management.
Join a Board of Advisors at my Alma Mater.	Meet with the Department Chair by 1 March.	Conceptualize approach for industry analysis.	Develop an industry analysis and include current market drivers, employment forecasts by graduate type and profile the top 10 corporations.	Work on documentation before and after normal work day and during lunch meetings to gather information and validate assumptions.	Seek feedback from industry and academic leaders, peers and management.
Be selected for Senior level career path.	Express an interest in being selected for advancement to Assoc. VP by 1 April.	Identify a minimum of three examples from the past three years that evidence my abilities and willingness to work at a higher level.	Document the money made or saved from the three examples from the past three years and include the impact on the organization.	Work on documentation before and after normal work day.	Seek recommendations from peers and upper level management regarding my performance.
Be elected an officer in the Medical Devices Industry Forum.	Meet with Forum leadership by 1 May.	Conceptualize platform for leadership role.	Create a one-page leadership statement.	Work on documentation before and after normal work day.	Seek feedback from Forum members, peers and management.
Be promoted from Ex. Director to Assoc. VP.	Discuss career path, opportunities for advancement and stretch assignments with my VP by 1 July.	Map out potential money-saving initiatives and ways to increase revenue and decrease costs.	Research, document and prioritize money-saving initiatives and ways to increase revenue and decrease costs.	Work on research and report preparation before and after normal work day.	Solicit input from peers in and outside the organization and cite them in the report.

Professional Development Goals

GOAL	OBJECTIVES	STRATEGIES	TACTICS	EFFORT EXPENDED	FOCUS ON RELATIONSHIPS
Accomplishment to be achieved.	Specific, measurable steps that have a completion date.	The "thinking" aspect involved in achieving your objectives.	The "doing" aspect involved in achieving a strategy.	Amount and quality of effort put forth.	Frequency and richness of engagement.
PROFESSIONAL DEVELOPMENT					
Obtain a Social Media Professional Certificate.	Complete the online self-paced program by 1 Nov.	Identify the ways in which a certificate in social media can impact my personal and professional goals.	Enroll in the program by March 1.	Complete course requirements before and after work and on the weekends.	Engage with my instructor and classmates on a regular basis. Connect on social media and stay in touch after we complete the program.
Be an active volunteer for the local Boys and Girls Club.	Begin volunteering by 1 June.	Identify the ways in which I can use my talents and connections to the benefit of the Boys and Girls Club and the children that aligns with my current career goals.	Meet with the volunteer coordinator and explore all of the options.	Meet during my lunch hour and after work.	Connect bi-weekly with the coordinator until I begin volunteering and weekly thereafter.
Maintain professional certifications not supported by my employer.	Complete bi-annual certification requirements by 1 Nov.	Explore alternate ways for achieving certification credits (e.g., serving as an instructor/other).	Compare certification requirement options with my capacity and goals.	Review, decide on, and pursue credits on the weekends.	Reach out to my peers who hold the same certification and ask how they earn credits.
Gain new knowledge, skills and abilities unrelated to my current position.	Determine the demand for a new local networking meet-up group by 1 Aug.	Identify the ways in which a local networking meet-up group could be beneficial to various groups throughout the community.	Research and meet with professionals throughout the community to understand what groups exist, what's been successful and what hasn't worked.	Research before and after work and meet during lunch and after work as necessary.	Update my connections periodically regarding the progress of this initiative.

Your Story Goals

GOAL	OBJECTIVES	STRATEGIES	TACTICS	EFFORT EXPENDED	FOCUS ON RELATIONSHIPS
Accomplishment to be achieved.	Specific, measurable steps that have a completion date.	The "thinking" aspect involved in achieving your objectives.	The "doing" aspect involved in achieving a strategy.	Amount and quality of effort put forth.	Frequency and richness of engagement.
YOUR STORY					
Write my story to reflect my knowledge, skills, abilities, values, passions, accomplishments, setbacks, interests and aspirations.	Complete a draft of my story by 1 March.	Reflect upon my answers to the exercises in this workbook and decide how I want to position myself in the market in the short and long term.	Complete the exercises in this workbook.	Work on the exercises in the workbook before and after work and on the weekends.	Seek feedback from my wife after I complete each section of exercises.
Refine my story and prepare it for distribution.	Complete my story by 1 May.	Decide who I will seek input from ensuring a well rounded representation from my past, present and anticipated future.	Create a schedule of who I will talk with weekly and work from that schedule until I have spoken with everyone.	Gather feedback after work, on the weekends and during lunches.	Seek feedback from those who have supported my development as well as those that I've received constructive criticism from in the past.
Use my story to create a positioning statement, elevator pitch and talking points.	Complete a positioning statement, elevator pitch and talking points by 15 May.	Reflect upon the various audiences that I will target and think about their needs, attributes and experiences.	Create personas for my target audiences and then create the positioning statement, elevator pitch and talking points.	Work on the personas, positioning statement, elevator pitch and talking points before and after work and on the weekends.	Seek feedback from my wife and peers and refine as needed.
Use my story and evaluate its effectiveness.	Use my story in my social media profiles online from 1 June to 1 Sept..	Think about the ways in which I can determine if I'm making progress toward my goals.	Create milestones and outcomes to guide and measure my performance.	Work on the milestones and outcomes before and after work and on the weekends.	Seek feedback from my peers and refine as needed.
Update my story bi-annually and as needed.	Update my story in January and June annually.	Reflect upon the ways in which I may be changing and how these changes impact my story.	Keep a journal to briefly note changes in my knowledge, skills, abilities, values, passions, accomplishments, setbacks, interests and aspirations.	Makes notes in my journal nightly.	Discuss changes with my wife monthly.

Your Brand Identity Goals

GOAL	OBJECTIVES	STRATEGIES	TACTICS	EFFORT EXPENDED	FOCUS ON RELATIONSHIPS
Accomplishment to be achieved.	Specific, measurable steps that have a completion date.	The "thinking" aspect involved in achieving your objectives.	The "doing" aspect involved in achieving a strategy.	Amount and quality of effort put forth.	Frequency and richness of engagement.
YOUR BRAND IDENTITY					
Use professional photographs on my social media profiles, blog, association profiles and for presentations and articles.	Obtain professional photographs by 1 March.	Reflect upon the best professional photographs I've seen during the past year.	Research samples and the photographers who took the photographs; obtain quotes and select a photographer and wardrobe.	Research before and after work and on the weekends.	Share the rationale for my personal branding plan briefly with everyone that I contact to request photographer information.
Use select fonts and colors to represent my brand.	Select fonts and colors by 1 March.	Decide what characteristics I want my fonts to represent and what emotions I want to evoke with color.	Research colors and fonts to understand what they represent and communicate.	Research before and after work and on the weekends.	Solicit input from a graphic designer and feedback from my wife and peers regarding my options and preferences.
Use select letterhead, envelopes, note cards, labels, business cards (independent of my employer) and a presentation template to represent my personal brand.	Obtain branded letterhead, envelopes, note cards, labels, business cards (independent of my employer) and a presentation template by 1 April.	Decide what emotions I want to evoke and what style I want to present.	Research stationary, business card trends, and use the information gathered regarding fonts and colors.	Research before and after work, at lunch and on the weekends.	Solicit input from a graphic designer and feedback from my wife and peers regarding my options and preferences.
Use a branded email signature, logo and brochure to represent my personal brand.	Obtain a branded email signature, logo and brochure by 1 April.	Decide what I want to communicate, emotions I want to evoke, and style I want to present.	Work with a freelance marketing consultant.	Connect as needed and draft copy and review feedback before and after work, at lunch and on the weekends.	Solicit input from a graphic designer and feedback from my wife and peers regarding my options and preferences.
Use a branded blog to establish my thought leadership and build my brand equity.	Launch my blog by 1 May.	Decide what I want to communicate, which emotions I want to evoke and the style I want to present.	Work with a web site design firm.	Connect as needed and draft copy and review feedback before and after work, at lunch and on the weekends.	Solicit feedback from my wife and peers and revise as necessary.

Social Media and Online Presence Goals

GOAL	OBJECTIVES	STRATEGIES	TACTICS	EFFORT EXPENDED	FOCUS ON RELATIONSHIPS
Accomplishment to be achieved.	Specific, measurable steps that have a completion date.	The "thinking" aspect involved in achieving your objectives.	The "doing" aspect involved in achieving a strategy.	Amount and quality of effort put forth.	Frequency and richness of engagement.
SOCIAL MEDIA AND ONLINE PRESENCE					
Understand my social media presence.	Audit my current social media presence by 1 March.	Reflect upon and determine the value I've added through social media.	Create a list of the social media sites I use and rank my use according to frequency and the richness of the engagement (e.g., one-way, two-way or group).	Compile information before and after work and on the weekends.	Discuss with my peers.
Establish professional presence on LinkedIn®, Facebook®, Twitter® and Google+®.	Create profiles on LinkedIn®, Facebook®, Twitter® and Google+® by 1 April.	Decide which social media sites are the most appropriate for me.	Read books, norms and setup guides and create profiles with consistent content on each site.	Compile information before and after work and on the weekends.	Seek input from my peers and others on social media regarding best practices.
Have an engaged, robust and diverse network on a variety of social media sites.	Invite peers and other professionals to connect with me by 1 May.	Determine which groups and organizations I want to associate with my personal brand.	Create a list of individuals from my past and current situation I'd like to engage with on social media.	Compile information before and after work and on the weekends.	Seek input from my peers and others on social media regarding best practices.
			Create an engagement plan with a timeline that forecasts a certain amount of time be dedicated to social media.		
			Create plans to measure my effectiveness according to a periodic timeline.		

Planning to Network: Insight

Organizations	Targets (Who You Seek to Meet)	Direct Connections (Your Contacts)	Bridges (Individuals Who Are Connected to Your Target)	Alternate Bridges or Connections	Insight (What is the connection?)
Becton Dickinson	Bill Jones, VP Planning Becton Dickinson	Alexander Smith, Indiana University Alumnus			Our children go to the same school
Smiths Medical	Sally Myers, Director Operations, Smiths Medical		Jill Weaver		We serve on the same United Way Committee
Cook Medical	Jan Fleming, Director of Manufacturing		Ross Townsend, Saint Mary-of-the-Woods College Alumnus		He went through the Master of Leadership Development program with my wife

Fictitious names listed above for illustration purposes

Planning to Network: Objectives

Organizations	Targets (Who You Seek to Meet)	Direct Connections (Your Contacts)	Bridges (Individuals Who Are Connected to Your Target)	Alternate Bridges or Connections	Objectives (What do you want to do/learn?)
Becton Dickinson	Bill Jones, VP Planning Becton Dickinson	Alexander Smith, Indiana University Alumnus			Industry insight
Smiths Medical	Sally Myers, Director Operations, Smiths Medical		Jill Weaver		Introduction
Cook Medical	Jan Fleming, Director of Manufacturing		Ross Townsend, Saint Mary-of-the-Woods College Alumnus		Introduction

Fictitious names listed above for illustration purposes

Networking Plan

Who You Will Connect With (Could be a direct connection, bridge or target)	How You Will Connect	When You Will Connect	Date Connection Made	Next Steps	Who You Will Connect With (Could be a direct connection, bridge or target)
Alexander Smith, Indiana University Alumnus	Via the Indiana University LinkedIn® Alumni Group. Personalize an invitation to connect and point out that in addition to both of you being IU Alumni, you understand your children go to the same school.	This week		Once connected, thank him for connecting and offer to put your network at his disposal should he be interested in connecting with anyone. After he responds, ask if he'd be willing to join you in a brief phone conversation.	Alexander Smith, Indiana University Alumni
Jill Weaver	In person or if you're unable to connect in person send an email Don't wait until the next United Way meeting	Prior to or after the next United Way meeting ask if she'd be interested in joining you for coffee/lunch		Schedule the coffee/lunch Afterward, thank her for meeting you	Jill Weaver
Jan Fleming	Ross Townsend introduces us via email	Next week		Schedule a coffee/lunch meeting	Jan Fleming

Fictitious names listed above for illustration purposes

2014 Marketing Goals

Goals:

1. Increase promotion and employment opportunities upon completion of the MBA program.

2. Position myself as a leader.

3. Leverage my network by working collaboratively with association members.

4. Increase my participation in the association and identify new leadership opportunities to advance my skills and abilities.

5. Use marketing tactics that are cost effective and reach the intended targets.

6. Increase the focus on my experience with the association and knowledge of the medical devices industry.

Objectives:

1. Grow reputation within the market, measuring progress using website analytics and downloads of my resume.

2. Expand my networking activities throughout the region by attending a minimum of two new networking events per month.

3. Grow my LinkedIn® network to 250.

4. Increase my attendance at association, alumni and networking group meetings by 10 percent.

5. Invest $1,000 in continuing education units this year.

6. Secure a minimum of 200 unique visitors to my blog monthly.

Strategies:

1. Reposition my brand using multichannel tactics and technology.

2. Implement my updated professional development plan and conduct quarterly progress reviews.

3. Interact with my network, association members, classmates and co-workers daily.

4. Promote my blog to new network members and attract regional media.

5. Share my story online and in person weekly.

6. Use my networking plan to increase and enrich my network significantly prior to graduation.

Marketing Goals

GOAL	OBJECTIVES	STRATEGIES	TACTICS	EFFORT EXPENDED	FOCUS ON RELATIONSHIPS
Accomplishment to be achieved.	Specific, measurable steps that have a completion date.	The "thinking" aspect involved in achieving your objectives.	The "doing" aspect involved in achieving a strategy.	Amount and quality of effort put forth.	Frequency and richness of engagement.
MARKETING GOALS					
Increase promotion and employment opportunities upon completion of the MBA program.	Expand my networking activities throughout the region by attending a minimum of two new networking events per month this year.	Use the networking planning sheets to identify bridges to my primary targets.	Interact with my network, association members, classmates, and co-workers daily.	Interaction is targeted and daily.	Engagement is daily and with a diverse group. Will connect and stay engaged both in person and online.
Position myself as a leader.	Increase my attendance at association, alumni and networking group meetings by 10 percent this year.	Use my networking plan to increase and enrich my network significantly prior to graduation.	Create a master calendar and plan when I will attend association, alumni and networking group meetings.	Interaction is targeted and monthly.	Engagement is daily and with a diverse group. Will connect and stay engaged both in person and online.
Leverage my network by working collaboratively with association members.	Grow reputation within the market measurable by website analytics. Increase downloads of my resume by 10% this year.	Promote my blog to new network members and attract regional media.	Welcome new members and include a link to my blog and social networks. Pursue guest post opportunities.	Research guest post opportunities before and after work and on the weekends.	Engagement is weekly if not daily. Will stay engaged both in person and online.
Increase my participation in the association and identify new leadership opportunities to advance my skills and abilities.	Grow my LinkedIn® network to 250 this year.	Reposition my brand using multichannel tactics and technology.	Meet with association leadership and members to identify opportunities.	Connect at meetings, online and after work.	Engagement is weekly if not daily. Will stay engaged both in person and online.

GOAL	OBJECTIVES	STRATEGIES	TACTICS	EFFORT EXPENDED	FOCUS ON RELATIONSHIPS
Use marketing tactics that are cost effective and reach the intended targets.	Secure a minimum of 200 unique visitors to my blog monthly this year.	Share my story online and in person weekly.	Encourage my network members to share my content.	Every few days.	Engage every few days if not daily.
Increase the focus on my experience with the association and knowledge of the medical devices industry.	Invest $1,000 in continuing education units this year.	Implement my updated professional development plan and conduct quarterly progress reviews.	Pursue speaking opportunities. Advocate for select affinity groups within the association.	Connect with association members and with professionals in the medical devices industry.	Engagement is weekly if not daily. Will stay engaged both in person and online.

Target Audiences:

Primary:

- Owners, executives, management and recruiters in medical device companies
- Indiana University Alumni
- Mid-Senior career level
- Passionate about the next generation of talent
- Passionate about the medical devices industry

Secondary:

- Association leadership and members
- Professionals in the medical devices industry

Target Source Markets:

Primary:

Indiana

Secondary:

Central Indiana Region

Top 10 Drivers:

1. Experience
2. Education
3. Association
4. Alumni Association
5. AA Affinity groups
6. Chamber of Commerce
7. Professional development experiences
8. Community involvement
9. Softball league
10. United Way

Industry Trends

Industry Trends:	Why market to owners, executives, management and recruiters as Primary Targets?
Discontent over increased regulation Global growth due to BRIC (Brazil, Russia, India, China) development Growing number of advocacy groups Several new partnerships throughout the state Increased foundation and corporate support	Owners and executives are direct access to employment Management can hire or recommend hiring Recruiters have direct access to those who hire
Emotional benefits of industry association:	What are owners, executives, management and recruiters looking for in an employee, peer or manager?
Altruistic motivation from improving and saving lives Contentment from interaction with like-minded professionals Satisfaction with and reinforcement of career choice	Collaborator Leadership Team player Work ethic and integrity Excellent communicator Experience working with diverse groups Self-motivated Agility Commitment to lifelong learning
What do my peers in the industry want?	*What can I deliver better than my competitors?*
Collaboration Leadership Less regulation Support for R & D Opportunities	Combination of experience, education and personal connection and commitment to the industry based upon my family experiences.

Connect to Serve

"Connect to Serve" represents a state of being. It's a way of learning, working and living. This marketing campaign implies that interacting with me is more than interacting with other professionals. It is an opportunity that assures meaningful interactions with each encounter based upon a deep passion for and commitment to the medical devices industry. I will launch my personal brand development plan and the "Connect to Serve" campaign in January 2014 on an in-state and regional basis. My campaign includes public relations, earned media, and interactive digital and email marketing supplemented by in-person networking and social media. My story and supporting messages are written to grab attention and motivate others to connect with me in person and online.

The job market today is fiercely competitive and I'm taking major steps to invest in communicating my uniqueness in the marketplace. The challenge resides in attracting and keeping attention even though executives and decision makers are more accessible today due to networking, social media and learning opportunities. The market is crowded and opportunities are limited. Increasingly professionals are accelerating the actions they take to get noticed, to come recommended, and to be the obvious choice for promotions and vacancies. My story and profiles are meant to attract and keep attention.

Creative execution: "Connect to Serve" features my story as a rural youth who moves to the big city after graduating from college to work for a startup medical devices company, only to discover that my 10-year-old sister back home has just been diagnosed with a rare and debilitating lung disease. My sister endures several treatments with varied levels of success. She finally undergoes a risky surgery that implants a medical device that improves her life. This happens as I'm completing my graduate studies while I work full-time at a medical devices startup. I re-affirm that my career will stay within this important industry and dedicate myself to learning, connecting with and engaging with other like-minded professionals.

The Always Serve message reinforces what it means to Connect to Serve: engaging with others to improve and save lives by pursuing careers in the medical devices industry. Always Serve presents me as a lifelong learner, leader and purposeful connector who is devoted to helping connect, inspire and uplift others. My campaign integrates social media, public relations and interactive digital and email marketing and highlights how I "Connect to Serve" daily in uncommon ways to uplift others.

The creative goal is to make this campaign unexpected and refreshing and connect with leaders' unmet need for a new generation of professionals committed to service before self, who are determined to pursue successful lives of significance. The marketing goal is to raise awareness and attract more opportunities from leaders and professionals who will invest their time and networks in mutually beneficial relationships with me.

Connect to Serve Message Points

Connect to Serve Brand Definition (What is Connect to Serve?)

Connect to Serve is about adding value to others' lives with professionals deciding to connect with me to network, learn and work together.

Connect to Serve Support Phrases:

- Value Added Connector
- Focused on Results
- Leader and Team Player

Always Serve

My Always Serve campaign tells the story of my commitment to the medical devices industry and how I lead and connect others. My story resonates with professionals who are committed to serving others. My story is shared on my blog and highlighted in my social media profiles, speaking engagements and volunteer opportunities.

Connect to Serve

- Always Serve represents a passion for helping connect and serve others.
- Connect to Serve brings meaning to Always Serve and makes it relevant for today's tech savvy and socially conscious, connected professionals.

My Unique Selling Points

- Current and Connected
- Savvy, Agile Collaborator
- Lifelong Learner
- Reliable, Resilient and Ready

Timeline

Tactic (activity)	JAN	FEB	MAR	APR	MAY	JUN	JULY	AUG	SEPT	OCT	NOV	DEC
Complete the exercises in this workbook.	X	X	X									
Create a schedule of who I will talk with weekly and work from that schedule until I have spoken with everyone.	X	X	X	X	X							
Create personas for my target audiences and then create the positioning statement, elevator pitch and talking points.	X	X	X	X	X							
Create milestones and outcomes to guide and measure my performance.						X	X	X				
Keep a journal to briefly notes changes in my knowledge, skills, abilities, values, passions, accomplishments, setbacks, interests and aspirations.	X					X						

Budget

Category	Cost
Professional Photographs	500
Graphic Designer	
Logo	700
Letterhead	200
Envelopes	100
Note Cards	100
Labels	50
Business Cards	100
Marketing Consultant/Freelancer	2,000
Brochure	
Printing	100
Web Design Firm	2,000
Site Design and Set-up	
WordPress Training	
Domain Name (annually)	120
Hosting Service (annually)	120
Search Engine Optimization & Site Registration	50
Books	100
Optional	**Estimates**
Business Cards (I use Moo.com®)	50
Note Cards (online provider)	50
Labels (online provider)	20
Briefcase	300
Portfolio	100
iPad®	600
Pens	100
Business Card Holder	50

Total $7,510*

*Assumes Internet connection and includes "Optional" elements

B

Personal Brand Development Plan Template

Tagline: _____

(NAME   ) PERSONAL BRAND DEVELOPMENT PLAN 2014

Table of Contents

Executive Summary

_____

_____

_____

_____

_____

_____

_____

_____

Story Summary

_____

_____

_____

_____

_____

_____

_____

_____

Career Goals

GOAL	OBJECTIVES	STRATEGIES	TACTICS	EFFORT EXPENDED	FOCUS ON RELATIONSHIPS
Accomplishment to be achieved.	Specific, measurable steps that have a completion date.	The "thinking" aspect involved in achieving your objectives.	The "doing" aspect involved in achieving a strategy.	Amount and quality of effort put forth.	Frequency and richness of engagement.
CAREER GOALS					

Professional Development Goals

GOAL	OBJECTIVES	STRATEGIES	TACTICS	EFFORT EXPENDED	FOCUS ON RELATIONSHIPS
Accomplishment to be achieved.	Specific, measurable steps that have a completion date.	The "thinking" aspect involved in achieving your objectives.	The "doing" aspect involved in achieving a strategy.	Amount and quality of effort put forth.	Frequency and richness of engagement.
PROFESSIONAL DEVELOPMENT					

Your Story Goals

GOAL	OBJECTIVES	STRATEGIES	TACTICS	EFFORT EXPENDED	FOCUS ON RELATIONSHIPS
Accomplishment to be achieved.	Specific, measurable steps that have a completion date.	The "thinking" aspect involved in achieving your objectives.	The "doing" aspect involved in achieving a strategy.	Amount and quality of effort put forth.	Frequency and richness of engagement.
YOUR STORY					

Your Brand Identity Goals

GOAL	OBJECTIVES	STRATEGIES	TACTICS	EFFORT EXPENDED	FOCUS ON RELATIONSHIPS
Accomplishment to be achieved.	Specific, measurable that are have a completion date.	The "thinking" aspect involved in achieving your objectives.	The "doing" aspect involved in achieving a strategy.	Amount and quality of effort put forth.	Frequency and richness of engagement.
YOUR BRAND IDENTITY					

Social Media and Online Presence Goals

GOAL	OBJECTIVES	STRATEGIES	TACTICS	EFFORT EXPENDED	FOCUS ON RELATIONSHIPS
Accomplishment to be achieved.	Specific, measurable steps that have a completion date.	The "thinking" aspect involved in achieving your objectives.	The "doing" aspect involved in achieving a strategy.	Amount and quality of effort put forth.	Frequency and richness of engagement.
SOCIAL MEDIA AND ONLINE PRESENCE					

Planning to Network: Insight

Organizations	Targets (Who You Seek to Meet)	Direct Connections (Your Contacts)	Bridges (Individuals Who Are Connected to Your Target)	Alternate Bridges or Connections	Insight (What is the connection?)

Planning to Network: Objectives

Organizations	Targets (Who You Seek to Meet)	Direct Connections (Your Contacts)	Bridges (Individuals Who Are Connected to Your Target)	Alternate Bridges or Connections	Objectives (What do you want to do/learn?)

Networking Plan

Who You Will Connect With (Could be a direct connection, bridge or target)	How You Will Connect	When You Will Connect	Date Connection Made	Next Steps

2014 Marketing Goals

Goals:

1. _____

2. _____

3. _____

4. _____

5. _____

6. _____

Objectives:

1. _____

2. _____

3. _____

4. _____

5. _____

6. _____

Strategies:

1. _____

2. _____

3. _____

4. _____

5. _____

6. _____

Marketing Goals

GOAL	OBJECTIVES	STRATEGIES	TACTICS	EFFORT EXPENDED	FOCUS ON RELATIONSHIPS
Accomplishment to be achieved.	Specific, measurable steps that have a completion date.	The "thinking" aspect involved in achieving your objectives.	The "doing" aspect involved in achieving a strategy.	Amount and quality of effort put forth.	Frequency and richness of engagement.
MARKETING GOALS					

Target Audiences:

Primary:

_____

_____

_____

_____

Secondary:

_____

_____

_____

_____

Target Source Markets:

Primary:

_____

Secondary:

_____

Top 10 Drivers:

_____

_____

_____

_____

_____

_____

_____

_____

Industry Trends

Industry Trends:	Why market to owners, executives, management and recruiters as Primary Targets?
_____ _____ _____ _____ _____ _____	_____ _____ _____ _____ _____ _____
Emotional benefits of industry association:	What are owners, executives, management and recruiters looking for in an employee, peer or manager?
_____ _____ _____ _____ _____ _____	_____ _____ _____ _____ _____ _____
What do my peers in the industry want?	What can I deliver better than my competitors?
_____ _____ _____ _____ _____ _____	_____ _____ _____ _____ _____ _____

(Marketing Campaign Title) _____

In the space below describe your marketing campaign. Review the example if you need assistance and consider what you want to be known for and which elements you will include in your marketing efforts. Also include the timeframe for launching your marketing campaign.

_____

_____

_____

_____

_____

_____

Then describe why you are taking the approach that you've decided upon.

_____

_____

_____

Next describe the creativity behind your campaign. Share elements of your story that you will use to connect with others.

_____

_____

_____

_____

_____

Lastly, describe the creative and marketing goals and how the message points you will use reinforce the main messages of your marketing campaign.

_____

_____

_____

_____

_____

_____

_____

(Campaign Title) Message Points

_____

_____

_____

(Campaign Title) Brand Definition

_____

_____

_____

(Campaign Title) Support Phrases:

_____

_____

_____

(Campaign Sub-title)

Describe the story your campaign will tell and where you will share your story.

_____

_____

_____

(Campaign Title)

What does your campaign represent?

_____

_____

_____

Who is your campaign designed for?

_____

_____

_____

My Unique Selling Points

_____

_____

_____

Timeline

Tactic (activity)	JAN	FEB	MAR	APR	MAY	JUN	JUL	AUG	SEPT	OCT	NOV	DEC

Budget

Category	Amount
Optional	**Estimates**

Total $ *

Assumes Internet connection and includes "Optional" elements

About the Author

Tuesday Strong writes on career management using proactive professional development and personal branding techniques leveraged by technology. Tuesday offers integrated solutions in career planning, goal setting, personal marketing plans and social networking strategies. With over 20 years of management, human resources and marketing experience, Tuesday offers guidance based upon a combination of her experience, education, and unique life. She challenges others to leverage their strengths and resources to prepare for success.

Tuesday holds a Bachelor of Science Degree in Human Resource Management from Saint Mary-of-the-Woods College, a Master of Science Degree in Human Resource Development from Indiana State University, a Master of Science Degree in Strategic Management, and a Master of Business Administration Degree from the Indiana University Kelley School of Business. Tuesday is a Certified Professional in Human Resources through the Human Resources Certification Institute. Tuesday completed the Management Development Program at Harvard University in Cambridge, Massachusetts. Learn more about Tuesday at http://tuesdaystrong.com.

www.ingramcontent.com/pod-product-compliance
Lightning Source LLC
Chambersburg PA
CBHW051411200326
41520CB00023B/7195